LESSONS FROM JOSHUA

GOD WHISPERS THROUGH AUTISM

Barbra Monroe Goggins

authorHOUSE®

AuthorHouse™
1663 Liberty Drive
Bloomington, IN 47403
www.authorhouse.com
Phone: 1-800-839-8640

This book is a work of non-fiction. Unless otherwise noted, the author and the publisher make no explicit guarantees as to the accuracy of the information contained in this book and in some cases, names of people and places have been altered to protect their privacy.

First published by AuthorHouse 1/25/2010

ISBN: 978-1-4490-7639-9 (sc)

Printed in the United States of America
Bloomington, Indiana

This book is printed on acid-free paper.

"Let the children alone, and do not hinder them from coming to me; for the kingdom of heaven belongs to such as these." Matthew 19:14 (NASB)

TABLE OF CONTENTS

INTRODUCTION

Joshua is my son. He lives with his older sister, Mona, a younger brother, Noah, and me. His father and I have been divorced for the majority of his life, so most of the time, Josh is around me, Mona, and Noah. He is my middle child, although he exhibits none of the attributes usually associated with middle child syndrome.

He doesn't feel the need to compete for attention or go with the flow. He makes his own path confidently, albeit quite loudly, and is adamant that he have your attention upon request. Joshua is bright in the areas he chooses to be and devious in many others. He knows how to get what he wants out of life and doesn't like to take no for an answer. When someone says no, it's almost as if he makes it his goal to prove them wrong. Josh can be very caring and loving when he wants to be. He lets only a select few into his world, but when he lets someone in, he doesn't want them to leave. Joshua has autism.

Raising a child with autism can be a truly eye-opening experience. Autism is an unexpected trip into something magnificent. It is difficult to explain how tremendously wonderful and very devastating it is. It fully embodies the clichéd emotional roller-coaster ride: the highs are so high that for a moment, life is perfect. You wouldn't want to heal your child if you could. And the lows... well, they can send you whizzing down an icy hill until you smash face-first into the rocks below. When you are low, the highs disappear without even a memory in the moment.

Lying facedown and hurting, it's hard to see anything but dirt.

But there is light. Really. I struggled to see it at first. After a while, I began to recognize, truly, the gift that God has given me. Faith plays an elemental role for me in bringing things into focus. The lessons in this book still have meaning apart from a faith in God, but without him, I found that I spent more time eating dirt than enjoying myself. And I did eat a lot of dirt, metaphorically speaking.

When Joshua was diagnosed with autism, I was a little despondent at first, unsure of what all that entailed. But despite my reservations at the beginning, I discovered more inside his little body than I ever could have imagined. He has taught me more than anyone else on the planet. He doesn't use words or draw pictures or paint masterpieces. He can't always tell me what he is thinking or what is wrong. Still, he has a message, and it is a message that his "disability" allows him to deliver. I believe that Joshua's autism is God's way of whispering to me every day, guiding me, making me a better person for my family and those around me. I work hard to hear what Josh had to say even though he doesn't use words like we know them. Navigating Josh's autism day to day unlocks a host of feelings and thoughts from the ride that I hopped on nine years ago. These are my highs. These are my lows. These are my lessons from Joshua.

This book is my journey. It embodies many of the lessons my son has taught me and continues to reinforce to this day. Joshua is how God chose to work in and on my life. The anecdotes and journal entries (*text in italics*) aren't necessarily in chronological order, but they are sorted more pertinently by what they demonstrate, as I'm never finished learning and practicing everything he has to teach. I hope I continue to be blessed with eyes to see everything Josh is trying to show me for many years to come.

Chapter 1

> "And we know that all things work together for good to them that love God, to them who are called according to his purpose." Romans 8:28 (KJV)

ACCEPTING CHANGE

Change is an inevitable part of life. God willing, we change and grow from infants into adults, spending our time changing our goals, changing our homes, changing our friends, changing our minds. Some changes pull us out of bad choices, but others aren't so welcome. Sometimes, change is thrust upon us. Maybe a loved one passes or we are fired from our job or we are forced to take a stand that makes us a little unpopular with our coworkers. No matter how hard we dig in our heels and resist, many times change can't be stopped.

Positive or negative, change demands our immediate attention. How we respond to these changes can influence the impact they make on our lives. The very essence of Joshua was change. I didn't always deal with these new adaptations in an appropriate manner. Sometimes, it caused me to focus more on the changes, what was missing, rather than on what was truly remarkable, and what these changes meant in God's plan.

Joshua challenged my original life plan and rewrote the script how I expected to live out my days. He altered how I handled parenthood and how I pictured it to be. He changed how I thought about the world around me and made me more prepared to accept changes beyond those that he handed me.

Every aspect of Joshua's life has brought with it some sort of a state of being beyond what was defined as typical. He was an unexpected pregnancy that landed me on bed rest at twenty-five weeks. Then he decided to stay two and a half weeks beyond his due date. He put me through fifty-two hours of contractions and arrived very unexpectedly after I was barely ready to push. He stopped breathing in the hospital and became the only almost-nine-pound baby in the NICU. Josh came home with a heart monitor and, after about two weeks home, screamed easily twelve hours a day. Joshua's very essence demanded from me a willingness to change.

Looking back at Joshua as an infant, I am sure that he wasn't one of the many kids who seem to develop autism after becoming a toddler. He was autistic since birth. Josh was very different. He didn't like to be touched or held and didn't seem to have a strong sucking reflex like most babies. He cried all of the time and had a very odd, vacant gaze. He wouldn't startle at noise.

When he was just two weeks old, he appeared to have developed colic. One afternoon, he screamed almost constantly from two o'clock until two o'clock in the morning, with only a handful of breaks for snoozing. But even sleep wouldn't last for ninety seconds before he would start in again. I tried feeding him, changing him, burping him, rolling knees to chest, driving him, swinging him, swaddling him, unswaddling him, swinging him, and still nothing.

Lyman, my husband, gave it a try, to no avail, and then handed him back to me. He seemed very good at ignoring the cries and going about his normal routine of playing video games and entertaining Mona while I fixed dinner. Josh continued to cry. I called the doctor's answering service, and she decided that with no fever or vomiting or outward signs of physical injury, it was probably colic. She scheduled an appointment with me for the morning and told me to have a nice evening.

Nice evening indeed. He cried through dinner and screamed incessantly while my husband and daughter went to bed for the evening. They seemed so peaceful, sleeping and dreaming while Joshua continued to bawl and shake. I tried to feed him his bedtime bottle; he would eat and whimper. Eat and whimper. Whimper and eat. I would no sooner burp him then he would start belting out a yell. I walked around the living room hoping he wasn't waking the neighbors in our little apartment unit.

Eleven passed, then twelve, then one, and he was still screaming. Nothing I did was working. I tried to lay him in his crib and snooze a little. He continued to cry and then started to sleep. I followed and closed my eyes while gazing at the giant red digital numbers announcing 1:57 AM.

I slept for the first time since three o'clock the previous morning. I started to dream until I heard another loud, shaky, piercing full-lung scream. My startled eyes popped open. Two after two. I cried right along with him. I tried to scoop him up and tried again feeding, burping, and changing the baby. I lifted him out of the crib and walked the hall again, hoping this time it would work.

I looked over at my daughter, who was still fast asleep in my room. My husband was asleep on the couch. No one seemed to be bothered by any of this except me. I was tired and tense with anger. I clenched my teeth harder and harder with every scream. He continued to yell regardless of what position I tried. I paced back and forth. He screamed louder.

I wasn't sure if I would ever sleep. I was sweaty and tired, but I was so tense my muscles were getting sore. I glanced over at my husband, who lay sleeping. He had slept through the night every night since we brought Josh home. I could feel my blood begin to boil.

Before we found out that Joshua was on his way, Lyman and I had planned to separate. When I found out I was pregnant, we tried to make things work. Our marriage was already rocky, and it wasn't helping that our surprise bundle of joy decided to try a scream marathon. I watched as my husband slept. Josh continued to wail until I snapped.

I ran over to my husband on the couch and pushed his shoulder. He awoke, startled, and I shoved Joshua angrily into his arms.

"Here! Take him! I can't do this anymore. Take him back where he came from. Take him back to the hospital! I'm done. Just take him back."

I ran out the back patio door and took a long walk around the pond to calm myself.

Of course, Lyman didn't take him away. It took a while, but in time, I began to accept the fact that Joshua was here to stay. He was calmer at night. My hormones began to level a bit. The heart monitor he had arrived with was returned. Josh and I began to bond steadily. I thought for the first time that our little family was going to be okay. But that little episode of colic frustration was only a swift premonition of what was to come.

Later, he wouldn't spoon feed. He couldn't sit up. He wasn't babbling, and he would sit and bounce in his chair by waving his right leg around in a circle. He would probably sit there all day if you would let him. The pediatrician suggested intervention, and I called a therapy group.

He had physical, occupational, developmental, and speech therapy. He had physical and developmental therapy once a week, and the OT and speech therapists came twice a week. Our apartment became a revolving door of therapists, all acting as a part of a "team" aimed at an early intervention process for Joshua to catch up to other kids his age.

He did learn to sit and crawl, although he was eleven months old when he did. He couldn't seem to pull himself up on furniture, stand, or walk. The exercises were difficult for him and were done religiously, and yet he was not progressing. At one point, the therapist couldn't assure me he would ever be able to. He wasn't advancing much in his other therapies either. It was then that we began to see other problems.

Josh began banging his head on the back of his high chair. Over and over again. I figured he would stop on his own when he figured out that it hurt, but he didn't. He would just continue to rock and hum E flat in one long, continuous breath.

Then, when speaking with the therapy group intake coordinator, I heard the phrase that marked the biggest change in my world and chilled me.

"Maybe we are looking at autism," she said.

Autism? I wasn't sure how to handle it at first. I had been a peer helper for my high school's life skills program and later worked in group homes during college. I had experienced a few students and residents with autism, but I couldn't imagine Joshua in that way.

Evidently, the other therapists had been discussing this already. They agreed that this might be something to look at with Joshua. I fought it for a while, partly out of fear and partly due to pressure from my husband to leave it alone. After a visit to our pediatrician, I couldn't ignore it any longer.

She showed me diagrams of when a typical child develops speech and various cognitive abilities. She charted dates where Josh developed some of the traits and circled all of the skills he had not developed yet. On some accomplishments, Josh didn't even fit on her chart. She wanted to check for a developmental delay. A psychologist came on a few occasions to interview me and observe Joshua and his behavior in different situations.

I was nervous. The questions seemed to be unending, one right after another: Will he follow directions? Does he respond to discipline? Are you consistent? Each question was like a piece of glass stuck in my skin. I felt like a horrible mother.

I couldn't believe how much my life was changing, all because of a six-letter word: autism. I thought the four-letter words were the bad ones. Spontaneity left for picture schedules and therapies. I had to watch the volume of my voice at all times and couldn't ever sing off key. Emotion had to be hidden when disciplining. Vacuuming had to be done when he was out of the house. I had trouble finding a sitter.

I didn't sign up for this ... dominated my thoughts. I remembered Josh as a newborn, looking at my long and lean baby. Holding my son, I had glimpses of a high school football star, a doctor, a lawyer. I dreamed how it would be teaching him how to ride a bike, skate, or play games. *So what now? I should change all that? But I'm not sure I can do this ...*

I am trapped in these walls. I wake up every morning in a surreal state, thinking that everything I went through was something that happened to somebody else. And then I see these walls. I know then this life is still mine. I don't think I will ever be free.

I am trying to love but I can't. Lyman makes it too hard. Our relationship is broken at best. I'm not even sure what is true anymore or what can be saved. Still each night, he returns to these walls.

I have beautiful children who need their mother. I am trying to enjoy my kids, but I can't. I try to put on a smile, but I feel like I am useless to anyone. I can't go very far away from these walls without Josh having an incident. Something is always too loud or too bright. So I stay here. Trying to play with the kids here inside these walls.

I can't go out, so they come here to do therapy with Josh. The pressure to do more with him just builds. Each session has more and more expectations and things to try. None of them seem to be working. Josh isn't responding. And I feel pushed and inadequate here in these walls.

Lyman seems to just like to deny that there is anything wrong at all. He'll just grow out of it and it will fix itself just like his trouble sitting up and walking. He thinks everything will effortlessly self adjust and there won't be any problems inside these walls.

So I try harder because no one else seems to have trouble with this. I have lost friends because I can't take the kids to see them. And I feel misunderstood by my family. They hear "autism" and don't know what to think. I don't have any words to help them. I'm learning myself. This is not fair. I wish I could escape this. Just get away. But I am with Josh each day and up with him three times each night with no real end in sight, no genuine answers. There is no room to rest inside these walls.

Those walls entrapped me for a few months. We were living in a small two-bedroom apartment with no room to spare. I was a stay-at-home mom with three small kids and in a highly strained relationship. Josh's diagnosis came about five months after the birth of his younger brother. I had barely gotten over the "baby blues" and felt very fragile. Anytime I tried to talk seriously to my husband about plans for Joshua, he would shut down and tell me that everything would be just fine, that he would grow out of it. And there was no more discussion.

Our relationship was already in trouble. We separated on two occasions for a few months at a stretch, not being able to agree on a true account of events. As crazy as it was, we kept trying. Because of my marriage, I had few friends to whom I could turn. I had no job at the time and no means of escape. The shadows on those eggshell-colored walls grew thicker. I wasn't sure where to turn.

One late night, I lay next to Joshua on the floor. Josh's eyes were closed, his little arm wrapped tightly in my long hair. He always had to feel my hair to fall asleep. I untangled him and propped my head on my hand. He was always so peaceful when he slept. It was the only time that there was any peace in the house.

He had moved to the edge of his pillow so his head was also on the floor. The floor was harder than the bed, but he preferred it. His therapist said that it was probably a sensory need. Josh most likely felt more pressure from gravity simply pulling him to the floor, while the bed was cushier. My eyes swelled with tears as I watched the moonlight kiss his cheek.

It wasn't from joy or sadness per se. It was more as if I were mourning. I was mourning the loss of the little boy I had pictured only a few years ago. I was saying good-bye to the quarterback, the reporter, the accountant, the father, and the grandkids. Part of me felt I had lost my child. In a way I had, but it was only the loss of my expectations of what my boy was going to be. I still had someone to love and nurture and teach. He was just a stranger. A tiny, deserving stranger who knew that he needed Mommy's hair wrapped around his chubby fingers if he was going to sleep.

Josh knew me better than I knew him. I felt like a failure. I felt stuck and thought no one was there to listen. Not many people are at two-thirty in the morning. I shifted my hand and tried to lie down. I felt a sharp poke at the nape of my neck. It was my cross necklace. So, I turned to God. I prayed honestly that night for the first time in years.

I awoke the next morning refreshed and renewed. The walls were the same eggshell white but seemed to be a little wider, and I notice the window in the corner for the first time.

After praying the night before, I had one thought flash into my head. It was of Mona and how she received Joshua those first few weeks. Mona was twelve and a half months older than Josh, the not-so-big big sister. Her reception of Joshua was far different from mine.

I was frazzled. He wasn't expected and Mona was still so young, although she was quite precocious. When he arrived from the hospital, he had a heart monitor with all sorts of wires and cords. He remained plugged into a box 24/7 and cried frequently. He cried even harder when you held him. I had trouble feeling any parental attachment to newborn Joshua.

Mona had a different take on Joshua's arrival. She played "little Mommy" from the time Josh came home. She was fascinated with him and how his bottles and diapers were littler than hers. She helped me change him by getting his diapers and wipes and powder. She didn't mind that he had wires and sensors stuck to his chest. She touched his head ever so gently and gave him unimaginably soft kisses. She looked beyond all that and saw her baby brother.

Even a month into life with Josh, when everyone else was wanting to quit, she still loved her brother. She didn't see a pest who was sucking up Mommy's time and energy that I could be using to play with her. She didn't feel pushed aside because the colic-stricken poop factory needed to be changed and burped again. She felt called to help her brother in distress.

One particular day I remember, Josh had cried most of the morning. Mona was patiently trying to put her ear up to the television to hear *Barney* and *Sesame Street*. I was starting to lose my cool. Mona tapped my thigh. I looked down at her. She was not upset or whiny. She simply smiled as she reached her arms up.

I started to get teary because I couldn't hold her. But as she ran and jumped onto the couch, I could see that wasn't what she had in mind. She sat on the sofa with her arms out wide.

"Ho' baby," she said with a grin.

I looked at her with surprise.

"You want to hold the baby?"

She nodded her head excitedly.

"He's fussy," I said, trying to discourage her.

She remained firm in her position, with her hands now grabbing.

"Ho' baby. Ho' baby!"

I moved Josh from my shoulder, got down on my knees, and placed Joshua, supported by my hands, into my daughter's arms. Mona smiled, and to my amazement, Joshua stopped crying.

In that moment of peace, I watched my daughter look in her baby brother's eyes. Josh wasn't a nuisance to her or a disturbance, but a person to love. She accepted him, wires, colic, and all, as her brother. She leaned in and so softly placed a kiss on his forehead.

I realized that I had a choice. I could be angry and disappointed. I could dwell on the unfairness. I could stay miserable and wallow in my self-pity, or I could accept Joshua, the changes, and the challenges that might go with him. I would never be able to help Joshua if I couldn't accept change. And things were going to change, more than I could ever have realized.

I found a job working evenings at a convenience store to bring in a little extra money. I wasn't happy with the way things in my world were turning out. My marriage was still in trouble, and I struggled to balance everything with three kids, one of whom needed more … much more than we were giving him at the time. My husband wasn't thrilled with me working but I didn't give him much of a choice. I offered to get a sitter but he said he could handle it.

One night, just like so many other evenings, I came home from work to find that Lyman was playing video games. I asked if he had done Joshua's therapy, and like always, he said yes. Somehow, I just never believed it.

One night on my way up the stairs, I kicked an empty toilet paper roll. It was the beginning of a trail leading to the master bedroom. I wound the tissue around my hand as I ascended the stairs. A rhythmic squeaking noise and light in the room made my pace quicken. "Oh, no," I thought. "He's rocking again."

I hurried. The more rocking Josh does, the further into himself he folds. I ran into the bedroom and stopped. My mouth gaped open as I surveyed the room: a toilet paper wigwam, a toothpaste mural on the bathroom mirror, water dripping on socks in the sink, air registers stuffed with shoes, drawers emptied on the floor, and one half-naked boy, who had tattooed himself with a brown marker, rocking hand to knee repeatedly on the bed.

It was obvious that Josh had been on his own upstairs for quite a while. I interrupted his rocking. A startled Joshua let out a shriek of excitement. He stopped and went right for my arms.

"Did you just realize I was home?" I held him in a big bear hug. He was wearing nothing but a diaper that was sagging and leaking down his leg.

"Ooooh. Let's get you changed." I laid him down on the bed and unfastened the diaper. His bottom was pinkish and irritated. I washed him gently with a wipe, powdered him, and put on a dry diaper. I dressed him in a clean tee shirt.

"There we go." He was smiling and looking into my eyes. "That's my little man."

His gaze soon drifted, and he was off in his own little world again. I went to the sink, got a washcloth with soap, and wet it. I wiped most of the marker from his face, hands, and belly before I noticed his knees. They were bleeding. I dabbed the washcloth on his legs. There were no cuts, just friction burns. He had rocked for so long that his knees were bloody.

"Oh, baby!" I grabbed him and pulled him down with me on the heap of covers on top of the bed. I kissed his forehead as he buried his sleepy eyes into my chest. "I'm going to make this better for you. I promise." Joshua fell fast asleep.

I wasn't sure exactly how I would do that. This was the first time I realized how intense his condition was and what exactly it might entail. I knew I couldn't stay and pretend everything was okay any longer. It was time for me to go.

I prayed the prayer I had used quite frequently to gain peace of mind, the Serenity Prayer, and then added my own ending for good measure: *God, grant me the serenity to accept the things I cannot change, the courage to change the things I can, and the wisdom to know the difference. Let my change follow your will, and should I make a mistake in discerning, God forgive me. Amen.*

Having Joshua in my life left me no option to eliminate change. Things were going to be different. He drove me closer to God, even if it was initially in desperation. I learned to pray and prayed hard. I had to accept Joshua in a positive light if I was going to be able to accept the changes and challenges autism brought. Learning to take him as he came was made easier when I thought of how God is accepting of me. I know that I am flawed and difficult to handle in my own right, yet he accepts me and welcomes me. Knowing that I have his acceptance makes it easier to walk on his path rather than my own.

Josh made me more aware of how my attitude affects how I can handle change. I'm more aware of others going through rough changes and excited for those receiving new blessings. Seeing God's plan in Josh's autism has allowed me to help deal with change in other aspects of my life as well. He made me realize that God can use even the negative changes or choices, which we've made on our own, to mold us and put us back in line with his plan.

Part of accepting change is switching gears from our own expectations to God's expectations. God has his plan and he is able to use the good and the bad to fulfill his plan. God wants us to have a childlike acceptance of changes in our lives. He wants us to say, "Okay. This seems unreasonable but I trust you, God."

God can use even the unexpected, heartbreaking changes to mold our lives according to his way. It becomes easier to accept these changes when we realize that even though our lives are topsy-turvy, God never changes. When I was finally able to accept this, it became easier to allow him to use change in my life as a way to guide me on his path, rather than me trying half-heartedly to drag him along mine.

CHAPTER 2

"...I tell you the truth, if you have faith as small as a mustard seed, you can say to this mountain, 'Move from here to there' and it will move. Nothing will be impossible for you." Matthew 17:20 (NIV)

HAVING FAITH

Faith is a hard concept to grasp at times. In our world today, the idea of faith is subjective. Some people equate faith with their religion, some see it more as a category describing spiritual beliefs, and still others use it as an emotion. Being able to recognize, accept, or nurture faith varies from person to person. For some people, the concept is a staple in their lives, and for others the search for faith is a longer process. Some, unfortunately, never experience faith in their lives.

I view faith in terms of my relationship with God. After you've relinquished control to God, you have to have faith that what he says he's going to do, he will do. The Bible says that "faith is being sure of what we hope for and certain of what we do not see." Hebrews 11:1 (NIV) To me having faith involves being assured that God will provide for me, even though there is no obvious way that would happen.

"How do you do it?" a neighbor asked while running into me at the grocery store. It didn't surprise me. I am asked this often when people find out I am a single mother of three children and one with autism.

My gut response is usually, "Not well!"

Then I have to stop and realize that what others are seeing isn't the apple juice spiked and shattered in aisle five, the missing shoe, and the barking every fourteen seconds. They don't notice I only used mascara on one eye because I kept getting interrupted. They don't notice the syrup from this morning's pancakes starting to rat my hair. They haven't heard the note of E flat hummed for the last hour and a half. They are seeing a mother who really cares for her children through the good, the bad, and the ugly. So when it is truly ugly, and even though inside I feel like I am melting, the superficially controlled outside is a reflection of my faith. I can only stop and wonder if they really understood how much effort the outside picture takes.

I've always had some sort of faith; sometimes, it was much stronger than others. There were even times I had almost no faith at all. I never denied that God existed, I would just assume at times that he had no need for me. I steadily wavered back and forth between recognition and disbelief. Joshua was the channel by which that faith was strengthened. He pushed me outside of my comfort zone. I constantly dealt with new situations and problems;

I had to decide what was best. Was I right? Was I wrong? Was I quick enough? Did I try hard enough? Josh created circumstances that kept me going or on call twenty-four hours a day.

Sometimes, Josh's progress would be slow. Therapy would get tedious, and I would be frustrated. I had trouble dealing with a collapsing marriage on top of everything else. I would get angry with God and the hand I had been dealt and decide that I was better off not having faith. Sometimes, I felt as if I was being dared to try it on my own. So I would. The times I went it alone were awful. There were no breaks. Turning away from God wasn't an option. I never knew what was around the corner. I needed help.

I was getting ready for work. I had started to dress Joshua when he pushed me away. He ran downstairs and started playing with his Leap Frog toy. He would play with the same storybook section repeatedly. It entertained him, so I figured I'd finish Josh last.

I dressed and changed Noah. He was set to go but I kept him in his crib. He was sleepy and was sound asleep after I turned on his mobile. I gave Mona fresh clothes that she put on. My daughter was looking through my make-up as I combed out my hair. Suddenly, we were startled to hear a man's voice yell up the stairs.

"Hello! Anybody home?" The voice was angry and curt. Mona and I ran downstairs to see a policeman in the family room. We stopped in the stairwell. The door was open.

"Are you missing anyone?"

I looked around downstairs. The table toy that Josh was playing with was upside down and playing itself. He wasn't in the kitchen.

"Oh, Josh!" I said as I looked at the cop. I started to go out the door to look for him, and the policeman stopped me.

"We found him. He was headed to 86th Street. A neighbor found him." He looked sternly at me.

"Oh, thank God. Where is he?" I started outside again. The officer put his hand on my shoulder to stop me.

"He's with your neighbor."

"Well, can I go get him?" I asked, confused.

He placed his hands on his hips and then took out a notebook. He took my name, Josh's name and age, and my phone number before grilling me with questions: "Why didn't you notice he was gone? Do you know your neighbor has had him for twenty minutes?"

I stuttered, "B-but I heard his toy. He was down here …" I glanced down at the upside-down Leap Frog toy that was playing itself.

"Obviously, he opened the door," interrupted the cop.

"I didn't know he could open a deadbolt!"

"Well, obviously he did. What were you doing?"

"I was getting ready for work. Getting my kids ready …"

He looked at Mona. "How many kids do you have?"

"Three. My daughter, Josh, and his brother." I sobbed. Nothing I had to say seemed to ease the policeman's mind that I wasn't neglecting Josh.

"And where would he be?" the officer asked.

"Upstairs sleeping." I went upstairs with the officer, upon his request, to show him Noah snoozing peacefully in his crib. We came back down and the officer headed for the door.

"Are you going to get Josh?" I asked.

"I don't really know yet," the officer said rudely. "Let me see how he is doing."

Mona, in a pivotal moment, threw herself on the policeman's leg. "Please, Joshy doesn't know. He doesn't understand. He's autistic. He can't talk."

The policeman looked at the little girl squeezing his leg and then over to me, who was now sobbing on the floor. "Is this true? Is he autistic?"

I nodded but couldn't muster any words. Mona released his leg and sat in my lap.

"Well, let me see how he is doing and I will let you know." The officer left the house.

I cried and hugged Mona tightly. I prayed. I was scared and unsure of what was going to be decided for me. I cried because Josh was gone, but I cried harder because I yearned for that half hour of him entertaining himself. All I had wanted was a little time just so I could get ready in peace. I felt guilty.

The officer came to the door, after what seemed like hours, with Josh in his arms. He had no shirt and no shoes. The boy with the blank face lit up when he saw me, and he gave me a giggle. I cried and snatched Joshua away from the policeman. He re-entered the house to finish up the report.

It was this day I realized how much I needed God in my life. I needed something supernatural to orchestrate my world. I couldn't do it alone. I had to learn to trust someone else to help.

Trust

Trust is a strong confidence in safety or results. To trust someone requires a grounded faith that this person has some sort of follow-through with his or her actions. A person gradually builds trust with another person, establishing a relationship built on good faith. Once trust is built, a person can have faith in another, believing that once something is said or asked, it will happen.

In working with Joshua (and many other children with autism), I learned that trust is an integral part of building a relationship. He has to learn that if he does what he is asked, he will get rewarded. He must first build trust with whomever he is working with before he will take it on good faith that there will always be a follow-through. Most of our intrapersonal relationships are like this. There has to be trust before any other relationship can be established.

This relational concept starts from infanthood, when we learn to depend on our parents for food, water, warmth, and shelter. We learn to trust (or not to trust) long before we can say the word. Usually, we learn instinctually to depend on our parents for basic physical and emotional needs. This is how God wants us to be with him: to seek him to provide for us. Still, many of us ask, "How can that happen when I'm not even sure he exists?"

A relationship with God is different, which is why religious concepts can be so much harder to accept than reject. One must believe in order to see, instead of the way we deal with other mortal beings. We must have faith in God before we can trust him. It is backward from everything we innately learned about people.

With God, it is impossible to see what he has done in your life if you don't believe in him. Without faith, you don't see or understand what he has given to you. You can't comprehend how he has affected your life. You can't picture what would be different in your life if you believed in God or not. You lack perspective in terms of how God might be operating in your life, whether you are a follower or not. We need faith before we can trust him. He doesn't love someone less because she doesn't know him; he simply longs for her to take that leap of faith.

One summer when Josh was seven, our neighborhood pool closed for repairs, so the whole family joined a different pool for the summer. It wasn't far. In fact, it was in the same neighborhood as my parents. Even so, it was still inconvenient. We had to plan pool trips, bringing everything we might need with us. Joshua had to learn new rules and resist the temptation of the concession stand. We also had to learn to handle crowds of people. It was an adjustment for everyone.

One of the rules Joshua had to get used to was that he wasn't allowed in the deep end while wearing a life jacket. The deep end was one of Josh's favorite places to be. The previous summer, Josh spent his time jumping from the side and popping up quickly to the surface. He enjoyed the free-falling feeling, but he always did it while wearing a life jacket. In fact, he never swam without one. He refused inner tubes, noodles, and swim wings. The only floatation help he would accept was the life jacket, and now it was causing him to be banned from the deep end.

He figured the rule out in decent time after I made him leave the pool after warning him about the rule. He seemed to understand after two days and looked longingly into the far end of the pool. I was shocked at how well he did while Mona swam in the deep end. He would watch, but he stayed within the boundaries.

He continued to follow the new rule for the next few weeks. He kept to himself in the area near the rope. He just looked at the kids swimming in the spot he wanted to be until it all became too much. He kicked to the ladder and got out of the pool. He walked toward the restrooms. I got out of the pool and followed. He quickly turned and ran full speed around to the other side of the pool. He shed his life jacket with two quick flicks of the hand and threw it to the ground as he ran. He headed to the deep end and took one graceful, soaring leap into the water.

I panicked and followed him, jumping in the deep end right behind him. I went toward the bottom to wait for him to sink and then noticed his feet were slightly above me. I surfaced to find Joshua swimming strongly across the pool. I was stunned and watched proudly as he swam to the wall. He beamed from ear to ear, knowing he was swimming in the deep end and following the rules. Josh was swimming unassisted, and he loved it.

I'm not sure if Joshua knew he could swim, but he knew he had a passion for water. When he jumped, he only had a strong desire to take off and start swimming. Having faith requires that strong desire—a desire to believe in something greater than yourself. The atheist would argue that if a desire is all you need, then God would actually be a figment of our desires. Not true. No man could create something that powerful. I know

I couldn't. Desire is only how we are awakened to what had been there all along. We need only to feel it with such passion that we are willing to take that leap.

Josh was a gift given to me to deepen my faith in God. He stirred that desire in me to seek out something stronger than I was. Without Joshua, my need for faith may not have been as great, and I may not have been as strong a believer as I am today. I may not have been able to pass a strong faith on to my children without having to face the special challenges that Joshua handed me.

I feel like God speaks to me through Joshua's autism. Maybe they were things that he was trying to tell me all along. I can't imagine trying to raise Joshua without involving God. Joshua showed me how having faith unlocks an ability to entrust God with every aspect of my life and allows me to trust that God will do what he promises. It took using something unknown—and a little scary—to draw this teetering child closer so she wouldn't fall again.

CHAPTER 3

"For what profit is it to a man if he gains the whole world, and loses his own soul?" Matthew 16:26 (NKJV)

RELINQUISHING CONTROL

To relinquish control is to release someone or something from one's charge. As it applies to our general society, it is often seen as surrender, a giving up of decision-making abilities, even just plain quitting. It would offer someone other than the one who released control the option of taking it. We view letting go as being weak. Surrender means loss.

Relinquishing control to God, in my eyes, is the most beautiful and freeing feeling I've ever experienced. Those who don't believe can do this too. They let someone else handle their problem for a while. There's nothing wrong with that; they get a break but they still must return to a position of control and take on the stress again. A mother teetering on exhaustion can ask her husband, a family member, or a friend to watch her children for some respite, but she ultimately must return to her position of control and again try to raise her family. If she chooses to relinquish control completely, she risks adding a burden of guilt, damaging her children's psyches, or even facing legal charges, depending on the situation.

Letting God control my life lifted the anxiety that my world had. Unfortunately for me, it was not something I was able to do overnight. It was a constant process of me grabbing on and letting go in an up-and-down battle. It was a long, chaotic walk that led me to the point of surrender.

After the policeman left, I was in shock. I had to get the kids to the sitter and myself to work. I finished dressing Josh, loaded the kids into the car, and headed to work. I didn't have much time to think. I'm still trying to digest everything that had just happened. I don't know whether or not my name is being given to a child welfare officer. He said he'd think about it. What's that supposed to mean? I take good care of him. I didn't know he could turn a deadbolt.

If that cop turns my name into CPS, Josh could actually be taken away. I don't know what I would do. I'm doing everything with him that I know to do. I'm tired of people not getting it. They see Josh and see that he is behind and a little slow, but they don't see that I am trying.

First his teachers, then his therapists, and now this cop? I feel like everyone thinks it is my fault that Josh is where he is. "Just keep doing his therapy and you'll see improvements." When? I'm doing everything I can, and no matter where I turn, I feel like someone is judging me. What am I doing wrong?

I'm in a new house, a new city, to start a new life. I need a new plan. I need God's plan.

I didn't really know what that plan was going to be. I knew I wanted to live a life pleasing to God, but I don't think I knew how Josh was going to be incorporated into that. Life with Joshua could be frustrating. If I wasn't frustrated with Josh, I was fed up with the people around him who were working with him or staring at him. I wasn't sure God's plan took into account trying to diminish my chances of a premature stroke, but I was positive that I was through with trying to meet the expectations of his early intervention team.

Josh was doing the therapies suggested and I was working with him several times a day, but he wasn't even making gains like other children with special needs. His interest in therapy activities dwindled quickly, and he often refused to participate with the therapists. He also picked up a new coping strategy: self-induced narcolepsy. Anytime Josh became stressed or overwhelmed, he would fall asleep.

Josh never quite fit the "plan." Children typically sit around certain ages, they walk and talk around fairly predictable times. Not Joshua. I felt guilty. Every time I would take him to the pediatrician, I would have to answer question after question in a negative manner. The questions were simply trying to chart his development, but they were comparing him on a chart that labeled him "developmentally delayed," and I felt crushed. I knew I was doing everything I could. Maybe it wasn't enough. Maybe I wasn't doing something right.

I felt like I had no control over my life anymore. In fact, I never knew how little control I had over my life until I had Joshua. I was constantly worrying over seeming simple things that I couldn't even answer: When could I go to bed? Would I sleep? How much sleep? Will I get a shower today? Can I grocery shop today? Will I have to leave the store? Will I get one item on my list or ten? Will I get to sit and eat? Will he scream? If so, how long? Will I get a shower today? Will it be a good day?

I had no control over some of the smallest things. No control in my life led to having no peace. I was tormented over everything regarding Joshua, from his therapy to his diet. I became discouraged.

It's late: 3:00 AM. I wish I were sleeping, but I'm watching Josh sway back and forth. It amazes me. He can't count, but he goes back and forth five times and then hits the floor twice. Sway, sway, sway, sway, sway, hit, hit. Over and over again. He's like a machine.

He never stops. He roams all day and all night. He doesn't sleep but four hours a day: two at the sitters and a couple at night. Constantly jumping and pacing and flapping and humming. Oh, dear God, the humming. I can't stand it anymore. I'm exhausted.

I work as much as I can with him, but I just feel it's not enough. Not much has changed with him. I can't afford private therapy, and we're on a waiting list a mile long for any other services. He isn't advancing. He has the mental age of a child fifteen months old. I'm not sure he will ever do any better at this rate.

I've been reading more about different therapies used for kids with autism. There are so many differing opinions.

Every doctor writing a book feels they have the answer. I've tried so much with him that has failed. A lactose- and gluten-free diet. Different styles of therapies. I'm not sure what he's supposed to be doing at this point. If there were anyone who could do a better job taking care of him, I'd probably let him go. I obviously suck at this.

Now he's stacking his books on the floor. Always in the same order. Red on the bottom, then the blue one, then the picture book, and Toy Story *always on the top. Now he is carrying them to the other side of the room. He drops them to the floor and restacks them. Red then blue then a picture book then* Toy Story. *I'm tired just watching him. I just wish he'd go to bed ...*

Josh was being Josh. He knew of no other way of existing. He was simply being who God made him to be: the genuine Joshua. What I grew to realize after watching one unusual ritual after another is that I would never have total control over who Joshua was. I could teach him manners, ways of acting, how to greet people, but I could never teach him not to be autistic. I could read to him or use nontraditional methods of communication, but it would not alter the person that God planned for him to be.

Josh was on God's time. Not only was he not developing the way a typical child might, but he wasn't responding the way many children with autism do either. And as ruffling as that might be to accept, that was the way it was going to be. If he was going to develop, how he was going to develop, and how much he would accomplish were not going to be rushed by any teacher, therapist, or even me.

Josh was under God's control. Accepting this was my first step to giving God charge over the rest of my life.

When Josh was six, we went to a school skating party with the whole family. Mona begged me to let her go. Noah was older and more independent; Josh's meds were more balanced, so I agreed.

At the rink, I started to regret agreeing to go. My daughter took off with her skates and immediately started to put them on. Joshua was scowling and holding his hands over his ears. I was juggling three pairs of skates, two nervous boys, and a diaper bag with all the necessities. We slowly made it to a bench.

I dropped my armful of gear into a heap in front of the bench. Even though Noah wanted his skates on right away, I started with Joshua, figuring he couldn't run away wearing ice skates. He stayed with his hands pressed to his ears as I tried to lace his skates. Noah was growing impatient. Another mother offered to help Noah with his skates. I agreed.

After I put my skates on, I thanked the mother and we scooted to the ice. The boys caught on quickly how to walk on the rubber carpets with their skates. We approached the ice. I set Noah up with a walker and he took off. Josh stepped on the ice and stood perfectly still. I slid him toward the walker and moved his hands to the sides. I held his hands on the walker and skated behind him.

He seemed to enjoy it at first. He had a tentative smile and would let me do the pushing. We went around the rink twice before Josh's skate hit a divot in the ice and he fell. I let go of the walker to tend to Josh, and the walker went drifting across the ice. I went to help him up.

Josh was frantic. He hated the feel of snow in the winter. (It was the only time of the year I could be certain he wouldn't run away.) He hated the cold on his skin, and the ice in the rink wasn't doing him any favors. As far as he was concerned, he had fallen into a hard bank of snow. He shrieked.

I anchored myself and helped him to his feet, brushing the frost from his pants. He stood with me for a few seconds, and we tried to skate. Even though he was doing fine, he was scared. He pulled himself closer to me and hugged my legs. I tried to console him but he became even more frightened. He was whimpering and grabbing my shirt. Right there in the middle of the ice rink, he began to climb me, digging his skates into my calves on his way up.

Joshua always climbed me when he was anxious. I guess me holding him calmed him down. I pulled him up and held him on my hip. My legs shook from the pain of being spurred and trying to stand with an extra sixty pounds in my arms. He was calmer now and nestled his head into my neck. I locked my hand around my wrist and held on tightly.

I nervously made gentle movements with my skates to turn and find the quickest way out. My body trembled as I balanced him and me on my skates. Josh looked up and smiled at me, and then he placed his head down again on my shoulder. I was suddenly cognizant of the fact that even though his mother was a less-than-amateur skater, he trusted me entirely to get us out of this little pickle. He held on loosely and was able to relax his own fears and his own concerns because he put me in charge. Joshua trusted me to get him to safety and back into a pair of tennis shoes. Heedless to the fact that my legs were shaking and people were whizzing by us on the ice, Josh trusted me completely.

I smiled a little. I was glad he could trust me. As I shuffled my feet, trying to reach the entrance, I felt a cold chill as I thought of how much responsibility that really was. He sought me, climbed me, and gave me control over the scenario. He just hung on and waited. I skated out the gate and placed Josh on his feet on the mat. He shuffled to the bench, reached under it, and handed me his sneakers.

I was pensive as I put on Josh's shoes. *Who am I supposed to hang on to when I start slipping?*

There wasn't any person who could fill my shoes. I didn't have many people willing to take over for me. The kids visited their father at least once a month, if not every other weekend, and I just took those days as my reprieve. I had offers from many different friends asking to help, but it was hard to trust.

I'd constantly wonder, "Are they serious? Do they know what they are getting into? Will they still speak to me afterward?" Sometimes, hearing how awful the evening went was harder than not going anywhere at all. It's hard hearing that you have the child no one wants to watch.

Our church frequently has small group Bible studies. The church as a whole chooses a topic and each group completes the study curriculum. Once when Josh was five, I was invited to join one of the groups. I always thought it would be fun, but never really considered how

I could do that with the kids. My parents already watched them when I had to work, and Lyman only took them every other weekend. The group leader assured me that he would be fine, that everyone in the group had small kids, and that one of them would act as the babysitter for the day during the group.

They left me no reason to say no, so the kids and I joined the Bible study. It was hard to let go and let someone else watch Joshua. I was nervous but I was assured everything would be fine. I enjoyed myself for a while, but when Sam, the sitter, came down the stairs without Joshua, I became nervous.

"Where's Josh?" I stood up from the couch.

"Relax," Sam said. "He went the other way around the circle."

I was nervous, but Josh did appear in the doorway in the kitchen.

"See? We're fine. You really can let me handle it," Sam joked.

I smiled. "I know."

The group went back to work. I relaxed some, enjoying the conversation. Later, Sam came down the stairs again. I watched for Josh to come around the other way again but saw nothing.

"Sam," I asked nervously. "Where's Josh?"

"He's …" He stopped as he was looking at the other entrance to the kitchen.

Before he could even tell me he had left, I saw the back door cracked open. I ran out to chase him. I wasn't sure which way he had gone and I took a guess, following the damp, mashed grass. I saw a small yellow and black speck in the distance and took off running across the open field at top speed. I finally caught up with Joshua, who was trying to swing on a jungle gym about three football fields away. He was upset that I had found him. I picked him up and carried him back to the house.

The walk back took longer than the sprint to the swing set. Josh wasn't happy and was biting his hand and punching my shoulder. I was frustrated and a little embarrassed. I hated for people to see my world firsthand. I didn't want them to know how often I have to drop what I'm doing and run after Josh. I didn't want them to know my house was equipped with a series of locks and chains. I didn't want them to see how often I have to take a punch, and I sure didn't want their pity.

I went back inside, tired and ready to go back home. The other group members tried to handle it in a joking matter, trying to break the tension, but you could tell they were a little scared. I smiled and nodded. Running hadn't been on my "to do" list for the day. It didn't look like going to the grocery store was going to go well either. I was ready to go back home and create a plan B: pizza.

I couldn't refute it. It was a part of accepting the change Joshua brought to my life. I had to realize that not every aspect of the day is under my control. Neither are the people who make up my day. I had to relinquish control to God (who was pretty much handling it anyway) rather than fretting over every move and regretting the outcomes. It is a sign of trust and faith in God to let him control the outcomes and guide your steps. I also saw it as a gift to me. I was given permission to relax and enjoy the child Joshua was. I know that if I do my part, I can be confident that God is handling the rest.

Flexibility is a way of offering God control. Being patient and open to a plan B or C (or even D) allows God to work in your life the way he intended. We might have an original plan, but we need to be ready and accepting of a change in plans.

Joshua demanded that I learn to be flexible, even before I was ready to give everything over to God. There were social events canceled, movies started and stopped, games disrupted, unfinished church sermons, days at the park rained on with tears, and trips to the grocery store aborted. I accepted my lack of control over Josh's behavior long before I was able to let God deal with it. As I came to the actualization that there weren't many people who could fill in for me, I began to do some soul-searching for answers. I knew God was supposed to be in control, but I always wondered how that really worked when you had a child like Joshua who wouldn't slow down for anyone.

When I was trying to control everything—therapy, at-home exercises, Josh's environment, a failed relationship, his siblings—I ended up able to control nothing. I felt more and more helpless. A woman at my church offered me advice; she simply told me to give it up to God.

I had heard this many times before and never felt it applied to me, because I could handle it. I should handle it. He didn't have to worry about me because I could take it. In my mind, it freed up his time for someone else. I just couldn't grasp his omnipotence. Josh brought me to a point where my ears were listening and my heart was open.

I decided that it was worth a shot. I wasn't doing such a smashing job on my own, so I gave total control over my world to God. I had nothing to lose. I was already losing Josh every other day, anyway. At this rate, I wasn't even sure he'd be alive in a year. I decided to let him be in charge and let him guide me in what was best for Joshua.

After that moment, I was free. I had someone there to catch me when I was sliding out of control. My anxiety was lifted, and I fixed my concentration on spending better time with my children. I was able to delight in more and worry less. We began to grow closer as a family, and the kids looked out for each other instead of battling each other.

God wants us to have him as a guide to free us from worry and to be a helping hand through all times, rough or smooth. When we allow him full access to our lives, God is able to stitch together good and bad events to fit his plan. God wants to be in charge of our lives so he can offer us what is on his table. We only have to be willing to let him in and trust that he is in control.

Chapter 4

> "Let your eyes look straight ahead, fix your gaze directly before you. Make level paths for your feet and take only ways that are firm." Proverbs 4:25–26 (NIV)

HEALTHY APATHY: FINDING FOCUS

Dictionary.com defines "apathy" as a "lack of interest in or concern for things that others find moving or exciting." Often when someone speaks about apathy, they instantly give it a negative connotation. Immediately, thoughts of brooding teens come to mind. Litterbugs. Radio-blasters. Anarchists. Apathy is generally perceived as just not caring.

However, apathy has a much more positive application. The truth is, apathy can be a beautiful gift that can soothe your mind and refocus your thoughts and actions to a certain goal or big picture. Healthy apathy is actually focusing on a task, situation, goal, or desired outcome to the exclusion of everything else.

Before I knew that Josh had autism, I got a little taste of what interesting quirks were on the horizon. Even when he was an infant, something just wasn't quite right. At four months old, Josh discovered his hand. He was always sucking on his fingers. None of this seemed too abnormal until he began to gag himself. This might have been amusing to me as well, if it had happened at home.

Josh discovered his gag reflex at the pediatrician's office. I propped him on my shoulder to try and ease his gagging. He would not stop. I would put his hands down, and he would push them back to his mouth. Over and over again. Gag. Baby smile. Gag. Baby smile. Moms were looking. Little kids expressed their disgust and delight, jeering and pointing. I was embarrassed and feeling very inadequate. I swaddled him in a blanket tightly so he could not reach his hands to his mouth.

"I guess I have the world's youngest bulimic," I said out of embarrassment. I didn't know how to respond. I felt like I had a responsibility to explain why I could not control my infant son. I had no idea how used to getting funny looks and headshakes I was going to have to be. I didn't know that more years would bring more stares and that it would get harder and harder to laugh them away.

I know they stare. I can feel them. Their hot eyes burn the tops of my cheeks. Their whispers carry through crowds. They always have something to say. "Why does she let him do that? She should teach him better." Those people make me

*furious. They don't know Josh. They don't know how he is;
it's not easy.*

*I know he looks normal, but he's not. I'm doing the best
I can, and sometimes I don't think anyone can see it. Not
his teachers. Not his therapists. I don't think my family does
either. What are you supposed to do when even the people
who are there to help you seem to be against you? I feel like
it is me and Josh against the world."*

I wrote that when Josh was three. It was a horribly
confusing time, trying to digest a diagnosis with a
developmental delay and balance another preschooler and
an infant. I remember how difficult it was sorting through
all the "help" I was given: what techniques worked in
teaching him, what didn't work, what were hokey old
wives' tales.

One of the problems was that there was very little that
worked with Joshua when he was younger. He couldn't
have cared less about therapy. In a standard therapy
session, the therapist would try different activities for
either his fine motor skills or cognitive skills and reward
each attempt with a reinforcer. He was motivated by food
but only for two or three trials in learning an activity. So
they tried different toys, flashlights, and bubbles. He liked
most of these, but they posed other problems. If the toy
was present, he would fixate on the toy and not participate
in the activity. If the toy was something Josh wanted, he
would become confused when the therapist hid it to use
as a reward and give up.

This was frustrating. It was frustrating for the
therapists, it was frustrating for his teachers at school,
and it was horribly frustrating for me. The entire team

was frustrated with Joshua's learning process, and we all had to come up with a new plan. That is when I first understood the difference between teaching a child with autism and raising a child with autism.

The difference was that the therapists could say, "I don't have any more ideas." Teachers could say, "I'm not sure what else I can do." They all could tell me, "We can't make him want to learn. We are at a standstill." They could say their piece and walk away. At the end of the day, they could go home to a house without Joshua (and all of his issues) in it. But I could not.

I couldn't walk away. I couldn't throw my hands up in the air and give up because when I would go home, Josh would be there waiting for me. He would run to me with those sticky little hands, reaching upward and using his only word over and over: "Mom-mom, mom-mom, mom-mom." He looked to me to help him during a period when I wasn't sure how I could. All I knew I could do was hold him, hug him, and love him.

Josh's kisses are so soft and gentle. When I hold him, he calms me, somehow, even when he is why I am upset. I try to do right by him, but I'm not always sure I am. I can't always tell by how he is doing. Is it enough?

His eyes are always searching, examining minute details is his little world. I'm not sure what he is looking at most of the time, but when he joins my world again and catches my gaze, I can see a little of what goes on in Joshyville.

His eyes are without fear. His stare is his strength. He isn't worried about therapy or school or if he can pick up tiny objects. He doesn't care about what others say about his learning or his behavior. He doesn't feel rushed or hurried to figure out our world. (I'm not even sure that he wants to!) He doesn't see how anyone on the "outside" thinks of him, and he doesn't seem to care. His eyes are blank until he sees me. I know Josh cares about me. I get to see a shine in Josh's eyes that I'm not sure he lets others see. I know there is so much more in there than anyone else sees. I love him just the way he is.

I had accepted Joshua as the child he was, right then in that moment. In that acceptance, I also gained an appreciation for his apathy. Josh did not care what his teachers said about him. He did not care that his therapists had no other ideas. He did not care that relatives thought he should be using coloring books and be potty trained. He did not care that people gawked at his eating skills in restaurants. He simply did not care. He had a beautiful, pure, healthy apathy that allowed him to be happy in his space. He had another focus. Now I needed one.

Unfortunately, raising a child with autism comes with a lot of unsolicited advice. I was focusing on all of the things in therapy that did not work. I was focusing on all of the advice and suggestions from teachers that were not helping Josh. I was focusing on failures and ideas of what I should do that didn't solve his problems. If I let them, these opinions were really going to drag me down. I needed to let go of the extraneous comments that did not affect our immediate task at hand: to make Josh better able to function in the world around him. I needed to follow Josh's healthy apathy.

Joshua did not take to spoon feeding at all. The OT told me he might have a spoon aversion. It was just a fancy way of saying he can't tolerate having a spoon in his mouth. It was one of his sensory issues. We tried plastic spoons, metal spoons, teeny-tiny spoons, curved spoons, and still no luck. The OT thought maybe we should try another object, like a straw or popsicle stick. That didn't work either. She then suggested using a chip or cracker to teach the spoon-feeding motion and giving it some time to see if he outgrew the aversion.

It worked well in the beginning. He loved to scoop his applesauce with his cheese crackers and really seemed to be getting the motion down. He used his cheese crackers to scoop everything: yogurt, spaghetti sauce, cereal, salad dressing. Unfortunately, the general public was not as enthused as I was that my son could scoop food onto a cracker. Going out to eat felt like we were an assault to basic decency. There was always someone ready to comment.

"You need to teach him better!" The words echoed from across the table.

I looked over at the woman across the table from us. She was cross and staring at Joshua, eating happily in his high chair. He was scooping applesauce with his cheese crackers and making a terrific mess of his face and the high chair tray.

I tried to ignore her and continue my dinner, but it was difficult. The strange woman kept looking over and giving her advice.

"You know he won't know what a spoon is if you don't give it to him," the woman interjected. My husband looked at me and gave Josh a spoon. Josh threw it down.

The woman gestured and said, "No, you have to put it in his hand and show him so he knows." My husband put another spoon in his hand and prepared a mouthful for Josh. He barely got it up to his mouth when Josh screamed, smacked his father's hand, and sent the spoon, applesauce and all, sliding across the floor.

The woman's eyes were open wide as she shook her head. "They need to teach him better."

Josh went right back to eating his cheese crackers and applesauce without his spoon and without regard to the woman at the other table. I lost my appetite.

I wasn't able to eat anymore, but Joshua wasn't fazed a bit. Even as young as two and a half, Josh was able to focus on what he wanted and exclude the opinions of others. He had a healthy sense of apathy that allowed him to enjoy the moment and not allow opinions of others to interfere. It wasn't simply ignorance. Our children hear and understand more than we think. He may not have heard or understood what the woman was saying, but he understood what his father was saying through his actions and persistence. He knew what a spoon was, and he knew it bothered his mouth. He just refused to let the outside world dictate to him what his plan was going to be.

I have to admire how he went back to his original goal (eating) regardless of the opinions of others (his father, the woman, myself). He kept his focus and stuck with his original plan. I still needed to be able to forgive those who gawked and to focus on a larger picture. I struggled for months trying to find a balance between isolating my family away from the public eye and making a scene everywhere we went.

Dear God,

Why do I always feel like I am being watched, every minute, every second? I loathe those eyes; they burn and ridicule. I can see right through them and know what they clench their jaws not to say. Their scowls say it all.

It's hard enough to have your son hit you, to slap the love right off of your face. I don't need to see those eyes. The judgmental eyes that now hold no respect for us and have turned evil. They are constantly dancing between pity and condemnation. Josh has lost credibility as a decent child, and I've lost my regard as an effective mother.

So my face stings long after he is calm. It throbs and swells my eyes. The outline of fingers streak my cheek, giving the piercing eyes something else to see. The walk afterward is like a walk of shame, but what did I do wrong? Even though it was just a hand, it felt more like a knife in the heart. Do they realize their stares are only stabbing me further?

I want to be left alone. I for once just want to make it through a day without a comment. I don't want to be the entertainment everywhere we go. Show me how I can be what you want me to be without me losing my mind. Please, make them stop staring.

Amen

The truth is that even though we pray for something, that isn't always what God has in store for us. No one ever quit staring. No one ever quit putting in their two cents. In fact, things on the outside of our family pretty much stayed the same, but slowly, I began to trust that God had a plan for all of this.

He had a plan for all of the rude comments, all of the stares, the sleepless nights, the occasional punch in anger, the lost tufts of hair. I wasn't sure where it was all headed, but I had to slow down and trust that God knew what he was doing. Once I reiterated that God was in control of my life, awkward situation became easier to handle. The truth is that I suddenly didn't care about what anyone else had to say.

Apathy was my way of being left alone when I couldn't go anywhere. I couldn't run away, I couldn't retaliate, I couldn't fight or argue. I was powerless until I allowed myself not to care. Once I didn't care, I wasn't as aware of the stares, and when they couldn't be ignored, offering to trade places with them usually sent them off in a full trot in another direction. Allowing myself to block the distractions made it much easier to calm an upset Joshua.

God is my big picture. In raising Joshua, I focus on helping Joshua function better in our nonautistic world. I understand that most onlookers aren't going to understand, and frankly, I don't care. I pray for guidance, the wisdom to know what is right for our family, and how I can incorporate my family into Josh's learning process.

Joshua brought me closer to God. Joshua is my reminder that he is my ultimate focus. When things get confusing or contradictory in my life, I ask myself if what I am doing is God's will. After that, I can become a little apathetic to everything else. Sometimes, I need to be.

Josh went a little crazy today at the park. He was very upset he had to wait on his brother. I could see him twitching from the back and covering his ears. I knew he was about to go off, but I still picked him up when he turned around.

He went right for my hair, yanking with one hand and smacking the back of my head with the other. He kept hitting me, over and over. Josh stopped hitting and ground his nails into my scalp. I wanted to cry, from pain and from all of the hot eyes I could feel staring at me. He then fell out on the floor, continuing his tantrum, pulling me down right along with him. My face was burning; embarrassed, hurting, mad … why does he do this to me?

I had to get him safely to the van so he could calm down. Just have to make it to the van…. I pressed my head to his stomach and pushed his hands to my scalp until he loosened his grip. When he let go, I backed up and allowed him to stand. When he did, I got him in a restraining hold and walked him to the car. The ten yards to the car felt like a mile and a half hike through gasps and horrified witnesses. I said nothing as he calmly climbed into the van. I hope no one had called the police.

Life with Josh can be a little nerve-racking sometimes. One minute he is a jovial kid, and the next he is angry and even a little scary. I don't always get support in public situations and really need an excuse to block out all of the other negative input. It is not a cop-out to accept bad behavior. I simply use it to shield myself from hurtful comments and glares as I am working to mold Joshua into the best person he can be. It is a God-given defense mechanism that I need and use daily.

Developing a sense of healthy apathy allowed me to cope well with the stares and questions of others, allowing me to focus on where I am trying to go with Joshua and God's plan. It may seem odd to see my off moments as such a blessing. What others would consider horribly embarrassing moments, I call training. I trained myself to filter out the unnecessary, hurtful comments and keep my composure. I am hoping that Josh has helped my other children cope with other areas of their lives by letting them learn that it's okay to apply a little apathy when needed. I know I wish I had been able to use this when I was younger.

Using healthy apathy shifts control away from those hindering us and places control back in God's hands. Over the years, Josh has given (and even now occasionally gives) me many chances to practice and perfect this skill. Josh automatically draws attention. Sometimes, it is good; other times, not so much. Regardless, wherever we go, we make an impression. And with a healthy dose of apathy, hopefully we show a little more of the strong, willing, happy family God would like us to be and a little less of the worried, timid, strained family that others and their comments can assign us to be.

CHAPTER 5

"Therefore do not worry about tomorrow, for tomorrow will worry about itself. Each day has enough trouble of its own." Matthew 6:34 (NIV)

SIMPLIFY

Well, it sounds simple enough. Make things less complicated. Get rid of extra stuff. Keep only what you need. Morning shows and talk shows have created a buzz about decluttering our space. Although reducing items in a physical space is one step to organizing a life, realistically, simplifying my life was a little more complicated than sorting out my closet.

Josh's very presence in my life demanded that I learn to simplify. Our world was a full body assault to his very being. Each one of his senses was on overload. He was highly sensitive to lights, sounds, touches, and tastes. Having autism meant that he could not tolerate the world outside without some sort of adaptation or buffer. I had to simplify not only the physical space in which we lived, but also my words, my actions, my thoughts, my expectations. Basically, I had to learn to simplify every aspect of my life.

Physical Space

When Josh was first diagnosed with autism, I was surprised to hear that simply existing in our world was bothersome to him. Sunlight could be too bright. His clothes or the labels could feel like wearing sandpaper. The sounds of vacuums or approaching planes could hurt his ears. Even the hum of the electrical wires around our apartment could be upsetting. I was overwhelmed at everything I would have to examine in Josh's world to help him function in the world. The therapist asked me a host of questions, attempting to discover what might be at the root of his fits. I felt like a suspect in an interrogation, fielding one question after another (and some, I think, more than once). Later, I wrote:

Another therapist came to the apartment today. They keep looking at his likes and dislikes and telling me he might have sensory issues. They tell me that his brain perceives and receives information from his senses differently than most kids. I just thought he was picky. They are talking autism as a diagnosis. I'm not sure what to think. I can't believe all of the things I have to look at in his environment just to keep him on an even keel. She kept asking questions for almost forty minutes about what he prefers with questions like:

"How does he do with loud sounds? Does he cover his ears? Does he make you cover his ears? Does he hear planes or thunder before you do? How does he react to household appliances? Vacuums? Hairdryers? Does he prefer dark

rooms or does he turn all of the lights on? Can he handle fluorescent lighting? Does he like toys that flash? How does he do in crowds? Does he seem affected by smells? Does he inappropriately sniff objects and/or people? Does he like to be touched? Does he like to be hugged tightly? Does he like to be tickled? Do clothing tags bother him? Can he wear fabrics other than cotton? Does he want to wear short sleeves or long? Pants or shorts? Does he try to carry large or heavy objects? Does he try to stack objects? Does he hide in tight spaces? Is he a picky eater? Can he tolerate a spoon? Can he eat without feeling his food? Do certain textures bother him? Too mushy? Too crunchy? Will he only eat foods of a certain variety? Just sweet? Just salty? Just soft?

And those are just the ones I remember. I am worn out. I'm worn out and I know we haven't even started yet. Everything and anything could send him into fits. The world doesn't seem to be made for Josh. I'm not sure we'll ever be able to leave the house again.

It was tedious, but I answered her questions one by one, and slowly we were able to get a better idea of how to help Josh just "be" in the world. She gave me ideas on how to simplify his environment so he wouldn't be overstimulated all of the time.

I began to adjust Josh's world so he could adapt to ours. He refused to wear headphones to mute noise like the therapist suggested. So I kept the volume on the TV low or turned it off to control the sound. I avoided vacuuming until his dad could take him on a walk. I only used cotton clothing and starting him on brushing therapy. I kept him away from fluorescent lights as much as possible and kept the house rather dark. I used room-temperature water to bathe him so he could adjust more easily to the water. I allowed him to sleep on the floor (which he fought to do anyway) instead of the bed for increased pressure on his body.

Gradually, I started to become pretty good at picking up on Josh's triggers. I watched him closely and kept notes to follow patterns. I learned what set him off and I became a little proactive in preventing his exposure to certain things, which changed his behavior at home. I slowly began to notice other patterns as well.

After Josh became mobile, he was unstoppable. He seemed to be bothered by things on the walls and would scale the couch or backs of chairs to pull the pictures down.

Josh enjoyed playing standing up. He would bring his toy or books to the coffee table and clear it off before setting his items down. And it was not done gently, but with an outstretched arm giving one swift sweep of any other objects on the table. Everything else around him would be in disarray, but the tabletop was clear for business. He would set his toy down and play. I think Josh was just trying to declutter his surroundings.

There were several décor adjustments. We slowly recognized, as things got destroyed, that he just functioned better in places with clear surfaces. It wasn't that he didn't like the items, he just didn't like them on the tables. Things on the floor apparently did not bother him at all. We removed knickknacks from tables and took the pictures down from the walls. The more open space he had, the better. Living in an uncluttered space is rehabilitating. An uncluttered home becomes a sanctuary from the crazy world outside, which is exactly what Josh was seeking.

Unfortunately, it was not enough to simplify his own space; Josh felt that other houses should be the same way. When we would visit family or friends, he would attempt to clear their tables and take pictures off of the wall. Occasionally, some of these attempts were successful. We avoided going to other houses and either invited friends to see us or were sure to keep our visits very brief.

Another pattern that involved his surroundings was color. Anytime Josh was wearing yellow or orange, he seemed more "connected" during therapy. He would make some eye contact with the therapist and even try some of the toys she would bring. But if the therapist or I wore bright clothing or if he sat on a red blanket to do therapy, he would be overwhelmed. Colors were affecting Josh just as much as the amount of light in the room. So Josh spent the next two years of his life dressed primarily in yellow and orange shirts. I stayed in neutral-colored clothing to not be distracting to him. I kept the blank whitish walls and beige carpet as they were. I tried to keep things for Josh as simple as possible.

Words and Actions

Before the therapist and I were sure what Josh really understood, she instructed me to keep my directions simple. I thought they were simple enough even though he never responded, but I needed to simplify them even more. When Josh and I did our therapy activities, I simplified the instructions. It was worth a try.

I started by saying, "Josh, put the block into the bucket."

Josh looked at the block and shoved it in his mouth.

"Ooh, yucky." I pulled the block out of his mouth and tried again with a simpler request. "Josh, block in bucket."

Josh smacked the block around the carpet for a while.

"Josh. In the bucket."

Nothing.

I touched his hand and then pointed inside the bucket. "In."

Josh put the block in the bucket and let go.

I smiled and rubbed his back. I stayed quiet while he continued to take the block out and then in and then out and in again. He hated excited praising, which most toddlers crave.

When I deal with Josh, I always have to keep it simple. Most definitely as he learns labels for items and actions in his world, I rely on single words and gestures to get Josh to understand and respond. I keep both words and actions simple, helping to define the object easily. I make sure my point is clear and that I am direct. Sometimes, I get so in the mode that I find I am speaking to my other children in that manner. The funny thing is that they respond better many times to a forward statement of what is expected. I always make sure to add a "please" or "thank you," but I make sure I get to the point.

Josh also had more success in therapy when he was presented with one activity, the task at hand. Having a choice would often upset him and cause him not to participate in anything. But when the therapist would only pull one item out of her bag, he would do more. She had to simplify her words to allow him to understand what was expected of him.

Now that he is in elementary school, Josh is able to handle being asked to perform more than one requirement before he gets a reinforcer. He does very well with a structured teaching environment that lists his activities on schedule that he must follow in order to get his reinforcer. For Joshua, this is usually some sort of break time that can include a snack, a toy, or a bike ride. Through the pictures placed on his schedule, he is able to see which activities he must accomplish and in what order so that he can take a break. Although he is doing more work than when he first started therapy, the schedule regulates him working on one activity at a time. On most days, he is able to be constructive, and the number of his tantrums has decreased.

Josh's work habits demonstrate to me how unrealistic I can be on myself. If Josh was given all of his task pictures in a bundle and his break pictures were revoked, he would not be able to finish more than one or two assignments before melting down. Listing required work on a schedule and inserting predictable breaks allows him to keep going and to be more productive. Josh's educational ethic is an id version of how our basic design as a human being was meant to be.

We feel we need to take on everything to be successful, and our world becomes a jumble of things we have to do. Even in our efforts to achieve order by sorting them in a calendar, we forget to stick in our "breaks." We don't take the time to reward ourselves with our own reinforcer, which could include a two- or three-minute brain break, a few minutes to stretch, a short walk, or a nap. I know when I overbook my life and continue without breaking, I don't always get everything done and feel like I've failed. I end up enjoying very little. I end up cheating my kids out of having me there happy and as a full person. We need to remember to insert "break cards" into our daily routine so we can be more productive and less likely to melt down.

Thoughts

In the early intervention process, it was hard to discern whether Josh *could* not communicate or *would* not communicate. Regardless, he was not communicating in any way other than yelling or biting. Using standard speech did not work. Attempts at sign were limited by Josh's preference to use only a few signs that were simple in dexterity. The speech therapist decided to get him on the PEC system. This is a picture exchange system designed to allow Josh to communicate his wants or needs.

The speech therapist came to our home one day with a handful of pictures she had taken of different foods Josh liked and of his favorite toys and activities. Even though they were all pictures of objects that Josh was familiar with, she never used more than two pictures at a time. This was done to limit confusion while he learned the system. If she presented too many pictures to him at the beginning, Josh could become frustrated and decide to communicate in an undesired way like screaming. He could also become distracted by another picture and fixate on that even though it didn't answer the therapist's question. (For example, handing her the picture of "watching video" when she wanted to know what he wanted for a snack.) Using just two pictures allowed him to understand what she was asking, and when the item on the card appeared, the picture had meaning.

I was working with Josh one evening when I decided to see what would happen if I dumped out all of his pictures. I watched Joshua's eyes shuffle back and forth over the sea of pictures. He was confused, and his little brow was furrowed in a much too manly manner. He whimpered and smacked his hands upon his knees. I then began eliminating pictures one by one and watched as Josh's tense expression relaxed. He was obviously calming down and was soon able to choose a snack. He picked the cereal card and munched happily on Honey Nut-Os. Josh was bogged down by all of his choices. He had too much to think about. He was frustrated that he could not make a decision.

I thought about how his need to simplify translated to the adult world as well. We get upset and nervous when we are handed too many things to do. We know what things we would rather be doing, and when there is a pile of work in front of us, we tend to fixate on something else.

Sometimes, choices overwhelm us. Freedom of choice is a great thing, and I hope that is never taken from us, but the reality is that we could use a little self-control. We react much the same way Josh does to things. We see so many things we could do or have, and we get overwhelmed. We overplan our time with things we want and have to do. We crowd our homes with so many things, we become suffocated by our own choices. Sometimes so much so that we forgot what our answer was to the initial question, "What was it we really needed?" We forget that our choices have a meaning and an impact, not only for us but also for those close to us.

Expectations

Special education programs exist to cater to the child with special needs. Educators do not expect them to be totally in line with general education classes and often adapt standard educational curriculum. One of the methods used to teach children with autism involves taking the task to be taught and breaking it down into individual steps that can be put on a list, either in pictures or in words. The student can then practice and learn each piece to be able to finish the expected task. This works with many of the tasks we have typically developing children do without thinking about how we taught them; e.g., brushing teeth, getting dressed, using the bathroom, jobs at school.

This also works when teaching academic concepts such as expressive language, shapes, colors, alphabet, and numbers and counting. After a teacher defines the expectation, the process to get to that point can be broken down into steps for the student to reach as little mini-milestones. This works to reduce the frustration of both the student and the teacher. The student is able to learn one piece at a time. The teacher is able to see each step fitting into the original expectation, and they can track student progress. Simplifying the expectation into reachable goals increases the ability to achieve.

As a parent, I had to use similar methods to teach Josh basic skills at home. I had to simplify my expectations and even change some of them.

Once Mona and Noah were getting their own drinks, I thought it would take a lot of busy work out of my day if Josh was able to get his own drink as well. I knew he was able to pour water from cup to cup in the bathroom and expected that he would be able to use a pitcher. I thought he should be able to get his own drink. It wasn't so easy.

Josh would always come in from school or playing outside very thirsty. He would always sign "drink" or hand me the cup picture. I decided to let him do it. I put a cup and a half-full pitcher of juice on the counter and let him try.

He looked at me funnily and then cooed, trying to move my hand to pour the drink. Josh was definitely tall enough, so I resisted.

"No," I said and shook my head. "Joshy do it."

He picked up the pitcher and began to pour his own drink. Before I could stop him, he had dumped the entire pitcher into the glass without thinking that it was too much. He took his glass of juice and left the kitchen, oblivious to the waterfall of apple juice creating a river in the kitchen.

I cleaned up the sticky mess and pondered what had gone wrong. He poured cups all of the time in the bathtub. It took me a while to realize that the problem was that I thought that pouring cups of water in a bathtub would transfer to pouring a pitcher in the kitchen. It did not. The cups of water were almost equivalent in size; he had no idea that the pitcher held much more than the cup.

Still desiring that he be able to get his own drink, I started in the bathtub. I added a pitcher to his next bath, allowed him to experiment with flooding the cups with too much water, and waited until he was reasonably able to control the flow of water. Within a week, Josh would fill both cups on the edge of the bath without spilling. He would then dump the remainder of the pitcher on his head. I prayed that the shower at the end would not transfer to the kitchen, and we tried the drink again the next day.

When Josh requested a drink, I again set out the pitcher and looked for an appropriate cup. Before I was able to set Josh up, he had found his own cup, a quart-size Tupperware container. This marked problem number two: the selection of glasses suitable for drinking. I had to break the task down into smaller, specifically ordered steps.

I started with making him select a glass out of the cabinet. Each time he wanted a drink, he had to get his own glass. Then I would pour it for him. Once he was successfully getting a cup or glass out of the cupboard, I made him get the pitcher of juice out of the fridge. Then I would help him pour the drink.

We continued to do this until he consistently did both steps independently. When he was thirsty, Josh would get a cup and juice, and then sign "more" repeatedly for me to pour it. I continued to hand-over-hand pour for a while so he understood that the pitcher goes back on the counter when you are done and not on your head. (I know, but what seems obvious to us isn't always so to Joshua.) After about a week, I decided to let him fly solo.

Josh came home from school signing "drink."

"Okay, Joshy do it."

He stared at me funny for a while, but when I didn't come into the kitchen, he grabbed a cup and placed it on the counter. He then opened the fridge and stood for a little while before grabbing the juice pitcher. He took the pitcher to the counter and poured his juice, stopping before he reached the top. He held the pitcher, and I nervously waited to see what happened next. He looked into the pitcher.

"Put on counter," I instructed, hoping a juice shower wasn't what he was debating.

Josh set the pitcher on the counter and took his juice to the table. I gave him a gentle kiss and a pat on the back.

Learning for Joshua often involves breaking down a task into graspable pieces. It was easier to simplify my expectations when I could redefine my idea of success. I had to view each piece as a success. If my success hinged on achieving one giant goal, I set Josh and myself up for disappointment.

Every summer I go through the toy boxes and closets, purging old clothes and toys, and every year I run into the same dilemma. I will find a toy that Noah has outgrown and won't play with anymore. I will start to throw it in the donation pile when one of two things strike me: Josh still plays with it, or he has not yet mastered the skill that the toy teaches. I have to weigh how age-appropriate the item is and if it is likely to teach him something functional. Sometimes, it is distressing because there are some things like twenty-four piece puzzles, which I am not sure he will ever do. There are other things I know he enjoys, but are way too beneath him, like anything involving the Teletubbies. Usually, I end up keeping toys in the hopes he will catch on to something new and even something unexpected.

It's a conflicting feeling when a younger child surpasses an older child by leaps and bounds in learning. On one hand, I get excited to see Noah flourishing and learning at an appropriate (and sometimes exceptional) rate. On the other hand, I feel a little sad that Josh isn't catching on to things at anywhere near a typical rate. I couldn't rush Josh in introducing new activities, and I wouldn't think of making Noah slow down. I could, however, divide my larger expectations into smaller goals so that Josh continued to develop further and I would be more encouraged.

One way I was able to simplify my expectations for Joshua was to quit using comparisons. Each child is an individual and on their own scale. Josh surprises me every day with something new he can do or in the way he reacts to something. He isn't going to do things in the same manner as his brother and sister, and he isn't going to fit on the pediatrician's guide chart of development milestones. He shows me every day that he is maturing and growing, steadily, in his own way.

I shifted my concentration from what Joshua can't or won't do to what he can or will do. I enjoy the moment and celebrate those activities that show his abilities. I refocus my efforts into taking the steps to reach other expectations with minimal frustration for him or myself.

Josh demanded I simplify everything: thoughts, words, actions, and our environment. Josh has shown me that all of the things I had to do to reach him are the same things I need to do in my life to become closer to God. Josh's autism-friendly world allowed me to place my focus on God by not being overloaded by radio, TV, and other distractions. I had to align my expectations for my life to what God was expecting.

We have a need to simplify our thinking and our expectations. It doesn't have to be so complex. For Josh, a good day is simply a day without disturbance: an ordinary day, nothing altered, no schedule change. When things do have to change, being able to handle it makes it a good day. Even if his peace and tranquility were ruined and his tolerance was low, a day with chocolate is always a good day. I needed to change my requirements to be satisfied.

Why do we as people require so much to have a good day? We tend to see our day in terms of events and happenings, and the more these events coordinate and go without flaw, the better. We wear ourselves out running around, trying to accomplish everything well, and in turn we succeed at nothing because we are so divided in time and energy. We run through the motions and pick up little enjoyment of the moment. We have an artificial view of how things are supposed to go, and often, we adhere to that model too strictly to be able to accept changes in the plan.

Most of us feel we have a need for a stronger relationship with God, but often our world is so full of stuff and our choices so overwhelming that we don't remember what his original request was: "Love the Lord your God with all your heart and with all your mind and with all your soul and with all your strength." (Mark 12:30 NIV) All of our things and options are getting in the way of our relationship with him. We need to have that "childlike faith." By simplifying my life and words, I was able to make more room for God in my life, with less distraction.

Josh demonstrates in his daily life that everything is done one step at a time. I can't expect that he will instantly understand how to wash his hands or watch for cars. Working with Joshua to develop his potential is similar to how God works with us: one step at a time. God doesn't expect us to become a religious figurehead overnight. God expects that we will come closer to him slowly. He doesn't expect us to fully comprehend everything at one time and start a new day in perfection. He even knows we will slip backward at times (some more than others), but he never compares our journey to anyone else's. God's expectations for us are simple, and he desires only that we keep trying. I know I won't be the person he wants me to be overnight, but I can take one step at a time. Each step I take, whether forward or backward, is only my own.

Constantly comparing is one of the downfalls to feeling successful in your life. Comparing material things, just like comparing abilities, puts the expectation of where you want to be further away. Someone will always earn more money, save more money, or spend more money than you will. It is discouraging when others are further ahead, and we get discouraged when there are no mini goals to reach or when our path is diverted. When things don't meet our expectations, we often become dissatisfied with our progress, our jobs, our families, and even ourselves. We may achieve some semblance of success, and then think we should be satisfied. We need to be satisfied in order to feel successful, but often there is a piece missing. We enter into a depressive cycle of unreasonable expectations, failure, and lack of satisfaction in our lives, which often pushes us further away from God.

He wants us to share his expectations for us and redefine success by his standards instead of financial wealth. He is happy with simple prayers and small steps toward him. God asks us to have a childlike faith because it is simple and pure, untainted by worldly complexities. Simplifying our whole being nurtures our spiritual being and invites a closer relationship to God.

Joshua has an innate attraction to the simple. Before Joshua, it was a concept I really didn't understand. I wasn't heavily materialistic, but I never understood why I shouldn't do more, say more, or have more. God used Josh's autism as a way to slow me down and force myself to change the way I was living. I had to get rid of the stuff, the thoughts, the emotions that were weighing me down, leaving me with only what I needed to move forward. Because of Joshua, I was able to detach myself from my things and attitudes that held me back from having true relationships with other people and with God.

CHAPTER 6

"With men *it is* impossible, but not with God; for with God all things are possible." Mark 10:27 (NKJV)

LIMITS

Everyone has limits. It is one of the complications of being mortal. Human beings have stopping points on what they can do physically, mentally, and even emotionally. Most of us innately know where our stopping points are and where, when, and how far we can go when we push these points. Are your limits your limits or God's limits for you?

I thought I knew mine. But Josh has shown me that what we thought were our limitations were often places where we simply decided to halt. Josh has pushed all of my limits, challenging me to go further, faster, longer. He has made me stronger, both mentally and physically. Often in his testing, Joshua brought me to prayer. Prayer prepared me for the limits God has set for me. Josh knows no limits. He has trouble understanding boundaries, and it takes many times of teaching in the moment for him to understand what is okay to do and what isn't okay to do. This can be a long, tedious process that not only pushes his limits of patience and ability, it also provokes my own physical and mental limits as well.

Early intervention. That's all I hear, day in and day out, with every therapist and doctor and teacher. I know it's important but I'm not sure I'm doing this right. Josh isn't progressing, and I'm told that doing as much as we can before he is five can make a huge difference. I'm doing the best I can but it doesn't seem to be enough. I seem to be doing the same things over and over with him, and he just doesn't get it. Coloring, puzzles, eating with a spoon; he can't do any of it. We are lucky to get through a store without losing him.

Private therapy didn't make much difference. Now he is not doing real well in his special preschool. Early intervention seems to be backfiring. The more structure he gets, the worse he seems to be. So what am I supposed to do? I feel like I'm running out of time to make him "functional." He'll be five soon, and I'm not sure what else I can do to help him. His peers seem so far ahead of him. They all seem to be growing and learning. Josh just isn't getting it.

I keep hearing how important it is to work with him at home. I just don't think anyone knows how much I try to do with him. If he doesn't learn anything soon, I guess that's it. I will have failed. I failed Joshua. He is totally dependent on me. He wants to be with me. He wants to play with me. He looks for me to teach him, and I failed.

I remember how much pressure I felt. We had moved to a new house and started him in a new school, a preschool program with special ed considerations. They stressed how much urgent attention was needed to help Joshua. They were unable to get him to do anything. He wouldn't imitate actions or look at pictures or sign. He ignored the majority of activities they wanted him to do. When his teacher would discuss his progress with me, I felt so inadequate. I always felt as if she thought I didn't work with him at home. I did. But he evidently needed more.

More of what? What else could I possibly give this child? I thought.

I was afraid I was out of energy and wasn't able to offer Joshua anything else. Fear accentuates limits. Our perceived limits become overwhelming when we are scared of the unknown or even nervous about expected negative events. We worry about our capabilities and if we can handle things or not and end up sabotaging our efforts to tackle the situation at hand. We are afraid of what might happen if we fail. We will also, out of fear, put more restrictions on ourselves. So, in turn, nothing is accomplished or nothing is accomplished well. We really don't know what we are capable of until we are in God's hands. God can push that envelope and make you surpass anything of which you thought you were capable.

Physical Limitations

Josh is quick. He is very physically able, is very strong, and has excellent gross motor skills. It used to be easy to keep up with Josh, but as he grew bigger and stronger, stopping the Tasmanian devil proved to be harder for me. I never quite knew how to prepare myself. I tried to always be on guard.

Every door in our house is on a keyed lock or deadbolt. So as a result, Josh became handy with a key. He would find one of several keys to our locks. He could rifle through a ring of keys, locate the correct one, put it in the lock, and pop the deadbolt. When he was able to escape at home, he would immediately run to our neighborhood fountain and take a swim. If he was playing in our fenced-in yard, he would hop the fence. If he could escape at church, he would seek to destroy the church's video library. If he got loose at the store, he would seek out candy or fruit snacks and open them before I could catch up. He still wasn't able to watch for cars or even understand that he could get hurt. I had to become quicker.

I needed to be stronger as well. Once I did catch him, he wasn't ready to listen, and I often needed to physically redirect him. Sometimes, I would need to be able to pick him up and carry him to a safer place. Even at what would seemingly be calmer times in public, Josh would develop periods of high anxiety and literally climb onto me until I held him. Basic care issues like haircuts, brushing teeth, and doctor checkups required me to be strong enough to restrain him. I had to build more muscle and endurance.

So I trained. I trained like I was taking on a marathon or fighting a heavyweight champion. I started an intense exercise routine. I woke up early every morning and did cardio and weight training. Playing with the kids outside, I would run a few wind sprints at a time or just chase Josh up and down the hill in the backyard.

Despite several naysayers, I was able to increase my strength and increase my speed so I could take care of Joshua. God gave me the boost in strength I needed to do the work he wanted me to do. Now I am able to catch him and even get ahead of him; I can run to stop Josh in his tracks, and I can prevent fountain diving, demolished videotapes, and opened boxes of food.

Mental Limitations

Building my strength took planning, the type of planning that almost everything in taking care of Joshua seems to involve. It's a continual thought process strategically weighing options and pros and cons of each move. Will he enjoy this? Can he endure that? How will I handle resistance? What will be effective? Are there any sensory triggers? Lights or noise? Can I do this with the other two kids? How close are we to a bathroom? If he throws a fit, what is the damage? It's a ridiculously exhausting chess game that somebody needs to call a draw to relieve the players.

Going at a crazy nonstop pace can take its toll. Not only can stress lower immunities and affect physical health, it can wear on mental health as well. I had been in a constant state of depression since I had Mona. Between an unhealthy marriage, hormonal issues, and lack of sleep, I felt I was slipping away a little more each day. After I left Lyman, I was happier but no less busy. I slept in forty-five-minute stretches and was becoming less able to function at work. The constant motion of day-to-day life with Josh was becoming dangerous for everyone in our house.

I thought he was dead. He didn't make a sound. I'm not sure how long we had been asleep but I awoke to a horrible crash. I thought a truck had hit the house, but when I peered over the edge of the bed, the VCR was missing, as well as the television and the chest of drawers. I sat up and saw that the entire tower had tipped over, and Joshua was underneath it all.

The lights were still on. I hopped up and ran to Josh. He was silent. I could only see his lower leg; his knee was pinned between a drawer and the top of the chest. I pushed the television to the side with my legs. The VCR fell clear of the chest, which was held up at an angle by two partially opened drawers. Josh's torso was untouched under the fallen bureau. I couldn't free his leg, now bleeding into my sock drawer. I crawled underneath and pushed the chest back with my back and held Joshua upside-down until I could move his leg. He whimpered a little, and I set him on the bed to check him out. He had a cut that zigzagged across his knee. He rubbed his knee a little and wiped the blood on my comforter. It didn't seem to be very deep and obviously didn't bother him much. He crawled back to his blanket, curled up, and went to sleep.

I doubt he was actually tired. Probably just scared, and the fright proved to be too much for him. He didn't appear hurt anywhere other than his knee. Evidently, he had woke up and made a staircase ladder out of the drawers to put in a movie. I was too tired to notice he had moved. Joshua must have quite a guardian angel. He could have died. And I would have been asleep when it happened.

I can't keep going like this. Everything is always about Joshua. I can't eat, I can't sleep, and Mona and Noah are constantly getting pushed aside because Josh is always into something. My kids are suffering. My work is suffering. I can't keep up with all the things I'm supposed to do because I'm always tired. It's not that I am incapable of doing my job, I just can't do it on two to three hours of sleep a night. I guess I should feel blessed having not crashed my car. I haven't slept for more than three hours at a stretch since Mona was born. At this point, I'm about four years short on sleep.

Everyone wants more, needs more from me. I'm doing everything I can, but I'm doing nothing well. I can't be a good mom, I can't catch up on my house, I can't be a good receptionist. I'm failing at everything. I get frustrated because not only do I feel like I'm failing Joshua, but I feel like I'm failing because of Joshua. I can't live my life fully because he needs so much, but he continues to need so much because I can't put myself fully into working on his needs. It's a horrible cycle with no end. I keep pushing myself, but if I can't sleep, I'm going to keep messing up at work. If I mess up, I'll lose my job. Then I won't be able to care for anyone. I can't push any farther. Last night it was overturned furniture; next time, he could escape from the house. Then I lose him. I don't know how long I can go before I drop.

I question my sanity sometimes. I go to extremes inside my fragile mind. One minute, I daydream about the police finding Joshua on another escapade and taking him to a group home; the next, I am formulating a new plan to get him to communicate. Other times, I think about throwing myself down the stairs just to maim myself. Then Lyman would have to take the kids, and no one would feel I hadn't done the best I could. Who does that to themselves? I don't have a choice to stop, but if I lose control, I will have nothing.

The cut on Josh's knee scarred. The scar bubbled and healed coarsely, reminding me of the many rough emotions that festered during that time. To this day, when I look at the scar's twists and turns, it reminds me of what lengths we can try to push ourselves. It reminds me how far Josh and I have come and how, when he is allowed in, God helps even the most jagged cuts to heal.

Spiritual Limitations

I am human, and sometimes human beings simply reach their end. I was at a point where I reached the end of my tolerance, the end of my strength, and the bottom of my faith. I became angry and impatient at the slow speed at which I felt God was working. I journaled frequently to try and make sense of things. I wasn't sure God was even listening anymore.

I feel like I'm falling without a net, dear God! Can't you see I am done? If I have anything left in me, then it is yours. I can do absolutely nothing else on my own. I am depleted. So if somewhere inside me I have peace, dredge it up for me. If I have strength, then show it, because I can't even drag my own feet. If I have any patience left, remind me where you put it. If I have courage to try something new, bring it … and a few new ideas, too. I don't know what I'm doing anymore. So if you think I can do this, then let me know how. I am tired and out of steam. Remind me where I'm supposed to be and blow me back there, please. Only you can handle this, Lord. It is way too much for me. Amen.

Looking back, this was one of the most desperate spiritual points in my life. I knew that God was real, I just didn't understand how he was going to be able to help my world. I tried to do everything alone and ended up drowning in my own negative energy. Being constantly drained physically, mentally, and spiritually kept me in a depressed state with unrealistic expectations of what I could do. Josh showed me how that I wasn't good enough on my own. I know that seems harsh, but it was real and essential for me to understand in order to be more that I was.

Josh has tested every limit I have: physical, mental, emotional. Even my spiritual limits were tested. Through his trials, I was able to strengthen mind, body, and soul. I wouldn't be the person I am today without learning to deal with Joshua. He showed me where my limits were on my own. Then he showed me how I could go beyond that with God's help: honestly letting God take over.

Limit testing drove me to a more consistent prayer life. I became more dependent on God to work through me so I could quit working on myself. I thought I knew what lines to draw and where, but those arbitrary lines left me anxious and unaccomplished. God lifted the fear that I was empty and hollow, and filled that void with his love. It stretched my limitations. I was more able to care for my family and myself. As I developed strength in body and mind, I was able to trust him more completely and realize that all things were possible with God.

CHAPTER 7

"Do nothing out of selfish ambition or vain conceit, but in humility consider others better than yourselves." Philippians 2:3 (NIV)

HUMILITY

Humility is the characteristic of being humble or modest about one's self-importance in relation to others. It is the acceptance of our true self and the deflating of ego. It is the epiphany that we aren't the center of world and the embracing of others. Humility is the realization that we can't do things on our own, and that we need other people, we need other relationships, and whether or not we want other people, we need God's help.

"Humiliation" is defined as the lowering of someone's pride or dignity. We tend to view it as something that is utterly embarrassing. Neither is viewed as a highly positive event, but a sense of humbleness can be derived from humiliating and embarrassing circumstances, even if it is not something that comes naturally for us. Through periods of humiliation, we can mold ourselves to be more humble individuals. Humility is when we take those embarrassing moments and instead of getting angry or sad, we reexamine ourselves and reposition our self-concept, taking ourselves down a notch or two.

Life with Josh invited embarrassing moments. They are assured of happening. Josh is an elementary-age child with the mental age of a toddler. He is focused almost entirely on himself, and he has an unregulated impulse drive. He wants to do what he wants and get what he wants when he wants it. It is a prescription for embarrassment, only Josh never sees it that way. I am the one who gets embarrassed.

Eating out with Joshua was always a big fiasco. It was almost as intricate as planning a wedding. Many questions had to be answered before we could consider dining at the establishment. Can he sit at a table near the wall or corner to prevent escape? Is the restaurant too loud? Can he eat shortly after arrival? Does he have to walk far from the door to an appropriate table? Can we pull blinds down if it is too bright? Are there foods available that he will eat? Does the table have a centerpiece, and can it be moved? Are there any plants or flowers within reach that he would try to eat?

This delicate balance of the real world and his sensory issues limited us basically to the backroom of buffet restaurants. This actually was a good compromise for our situation, except for the fact that it usually involved a longer walk to the table. Josh wasn't very patient and even less so when he was a preschooler. The walk wasn't a huge deal, except that Josh loved to dart away, and that could make our entrance a little spectacular at times.

One Sunday after church, when Josh was four, my father and mother offered to take the children and me out to eat. We tossed ideas around for restaurants and selected the Chinese Buffet for lunch. My father went in ahead of us to reserve a table. He soon returned to the front door and we all walked inside.

After the door shut behind us, Josh became squirrelly. He kept trying to pull my hand and drag me to the buffet tables. He smelled the food and was ready to eat. I reminded him several times that we were going to eat and that we had to sit first. He didn't want to wait. He continued hanging on my arm.

My father pointed us to our table and we began to walk forward. Suddenly, I felt a jerking on my arm that made me stumble to the side. Josh had succeeded in pulling me toward an occupied table. I attempted to yank him toward me. He quickly smashed his hand into an unsuspecting lady's plate of fried rice. I pulled him back, a split second too late. Josh ate the handful of rice happily as I apologized to the horrified woman.

"I am so, so, sorry," I pleaded. "He just gets carried away sometimes."

The woman stared at me, disgusted. I didn't blame her. I would be a bit put off too if some weird kid stole my food at a restaurant.

"Can I please go get you another plate?" I asked, holding Josh securely between my knees.

She crinkled her brow and remained silent.

"It's the least I could do. I ... I'm so sorry," I stuttered.

Josh continued to chew his rice and smeared the rest on my pants leg.

The woman shook her head and mumbled, "It's fine."

"I'm really sorry," I repeated.

I quickly turned from the glaring woman and picked Josh up into my arms. I walked to the buffet and got Josh his own bowl of rice. I walked to the back room sheepishly and tried not to return the glares of the other guests. I set Josh down and he found his seat at the table, anxiously awaiting his lunch. He ate eagerly with no regrets.

Embarrassment is humiliation. It is caused by caring greatly about what others are thinking of us or our actions. Humiliating experiences often humble us because we are exposed for what we are. This becomes harder if we haven't yet accepted our real self—a flawed self. Humility is the process of learning through our mistakes. Without humility, there is no learning, only a repetition of unproductive behavior.

One such self-defeating action is living the mantra of "It's not fair!" If this is your gut reaction to a situation, God may be trying to humble you. When there isn't one specific party wronging you (and even sometimes when there is), God might be trying to tell you something. The first step to humbling yourself is to own up to your own actions and choices. Otherwise, you are pointing fingers at everyone but yourself.

After changing formula and removing Josh's heart monitor, his screaming fits began to lessen and shorten in duration. My nerves were still shot and not calming very quickly. He would be more serene most of the times but have massive fits when his diaper was changed. I tried warming the wipes, warming the diaper, warming my hands, and even changing him under a blanket, but the whole process would send him into a meltdown.

One day, I had taken all the bad news I could handle. Our family unexpectedly needed to move, and Lyman reported that we had been turned down for several apartments we thought we could try. Mona was teething and cranky and chewing every piece of furniture we owned. I was feeding the baby, and I couldn't seem to get her to stop.

Josh needed to be changed shortly after his feeding. I placed the pad in the crib and laid him on top of it. I gathered my supplies and made sure my hands were warm. He seemed calm at first, but the very moment I unsnapped his pajamas, he began to scream. It was louder and harder as I undressed him. By the time I unfastened the diaper, he was red and mad. The only quiet moments as I changed the diaper were the points at which he needed to inhale. I finished wiping him and removing the old diaper. I quickly put on a new one and raced to dress him. It was all over rather quickly, but Josh didn't think so. He continued to scream. Mona entered my bedroom to see what was wrong.

Five minutes later, he had not stopped crying. I started to cry. I thought we were past the marathon scream sessions. I couldn't go through all of this again.

"Shhhh," I said, rocking him back and forth, patting his backside.

He didn't stop. In fact, he got louder.

"Shhhh! Joshy, you've got to stop," I coaxed firmly. My body was tense. I knew he could sense it and would never calm then. I removed the pad and placed him back into the crib. He continued to cry.

"Joshy," I said, shaking. He cried louder.

I went to touch him and stroke his tummy, thinking he might be gassy even though he had burped well after his bottle. He jerked and screamed louder, kicking his little feet as if to run.

"Would you shut up?" I yelled at the baby as I placed both hands on either side of him on the mattress. He cried and I shivered, using every ounce of energy I had not to shake him.

I felt as if my body was pushed back and I flopped down on my bed. The only thought in my head was *leave.* So I did. I ran past Mona and into her room. My anger was building, and I felt adrenaline rush through my veins. I picked up the makeshift Rubbermaid toy box and heaved it into the wall, toys and all. I felt the rush leave my body and started to cry. I cried about as hard as Joshua did.

I cried about what I had almost done to my baby and cried harder that someone had pulled me away. I cried about the mess I had made and the ten-inch hole in the wall that remained as evidence of my sunny afternoon. I dreaded what Lyman would say. I cried more when I saw that Mona had witnessed her mother acting like a lunatic. I couldn't stop my tears.

Mona disappeared for a moment. I was afraid I had scared her. She soon returned with a smile and came running toward me. I thought she was going to sit on my lap, but she stopped.

"Yeah, okay, Mommy," she comforted me, patting me on the head and shoving a pacifier in my mouth.

I smiled and pulled her in for a hug. Soon I realized that the apartment was quiet. I ran in to check on Joshua in his crib. He was quiet and examining his mobile with a startled look frozen onto his face. I thought it was rather odd until it dawned on me that the crashing sound had scared Joshua. He was finally able to respond to noise.

Many days and nights were spent in tears dealing with Joshua, even before I discovered that Joshua had autism. I never cried much before I had children. I had many opportunities, I just could never muster enough genuine emotion to do it. Josh taught me how to cry, how to just drop down to the floor and let go. He made me collapse into nothing. Life with Joshua was riddled with numerous humiliating and humbling experiences that broke down any false sense of pride.

Even simply getting a diagnosis for Josh was humbling. Autism was no longer something that happened to other families, it happened to me. I wrestled with feeling cheated and misled. Getting a label such as autism didn't work like a bandage or make anything better. It spurred a whole period of questioning, blaming, and mourning.

I don't understand what happened. Autism. I thought it was supposed to be rare. I feel confused, distant. I don't understand where I went wrong. Was it something I did?

No one seems to know why autism happens. Maybe it's genetic, maybe not. We've been through so many tests. I feel an odd sense of failure that I couldn't prevent this. This wasn't part of the plan. Do I feel like this because I couldn't stop it or because I have no idea what to do? Now what?

Part of humility is being able to accept the unexplained. I had to quit guessing and figuring and just accept that not everything was under my control and no amount of speculation was going to solve my problem. Grilling myself on what could have caused Joshua's autism wasn't going to make anything any easier. I had to trust that my life was in God's hands. Humbleness is accepting that God has his hand in things and willingly take his assistance. Whether we accept it or not, he still has his hands in our lives.

Although early on Josh never noticed himself in the mirror, an older, more aware four-and-a-half-year-old Josh loved to spend hours dancing and flapping with his reflections. At our new house, he especially loved the mirror above the vanity in the master bathroom. It was a giant four-foot-by-six entertainment center for him. Josh loved to stand at the side of the vanity and hop forward as if he were playing peekaboo with himself. He would jump and then suddenly stop and press his head against the glass. I guarded the water as he played his jumping game.

One day, he got a little overexcited about his new haircut and began to push on his reflected face. He laughed at his buzz cut and touched the image over and over. He continued to push harder and harder. Before I could even speak to try to calm him, I heard a loud, hollow THUNK.

The mirror had broken free from the anchor on one corner and had hit the counter. The weight of the monstrosity pulled the other corners directly out of the wall.

"Josh!" I screamed.

The mirror began to fall forward. I ran to push Josh out of the way, but the mirror fell too fast and I retreated out of instinct.

Crash! The mirror fell to the counter and down to the floor, shattering in a shower of glass. I squinted and turned away. It was quiet.

"Josh!" I yelled, panicked. I started breathing funny and became light-headed.

Just then, I saw a little bald head peeping up from around the wood and paper backing. He stood up and turned around. His face was blank but remarkably not bloody.

"Joshy, wait. Don't move." He froze and reached his arms up to me. I stepped cautiously on the broken glass. It crunched, feeling bumpy through my shoes. I was able to reach him within a few steps, carry him to safety, and place him on my bed. I checked his feet and body for cuts and bruises. Nothing. His head was clear of bumps. I gave him a huge hug and kiss and then let him go. He immediately curled up under the cover and placed his head underneath.

I grabbed a box from the closet and began cleaning up the mess. The carpet in the bedroom sparkled with glass shards. I walked around the corner and began cautiously picking up pieces from the bathroom floor. The shards were like daggers: long, heavy, and sharp. I put them in the box. There were two large pieces that were a few feet long that I took directly to the garbage can in the garage. I lifted the wood frame and loosened the glass hanging from it. It hung down like stalactites in a cave and intruded in the space where I thought Joshua had been hiding. The pieces fragmented on the floor as I moved the wood aside.

I checked on Josh, who was still hiding under the cover. He was awake but still in shock. He yanked the cover over his face again. I had filled the box with glass and carried it to the garage. It weighed as much as Joshua did—a good forty pounds. There was no way he should be okay. Josh should have been injured. The thought of him bleeding internally came to mind. But when I returned to check on him, he was using the bed as a trampoline and giggling as if he were with an imaginary friend. I figured he was going to be just fine. Miraculously, he was unscathed.

Even if Josh was in a tiny ball, he should have been cut. Yet somehow, he wasn't. I have to humbly admit that none of it was because of me. I could not save Josh from the mirror even though I could see the whole thing falling. I started in to help him, but my mother bear instinct wasn't as strong as the reflex to keep myself out of danger. To his credit, God had his hand over Joshua and kept him safe when I could not.

Because of his autism, Joshua has a natural sense of humility. Sure, he might be headstrong and opinionated, and enjoy getting his way, but he never thinks of himself as better than someone else. He may try to steal food but he never tries to take credit for someone else's deeds or accomplishments. Being nonverbal gives him an edge in living a humble life.

Few things are more humbling than silence—not an elective quiet, but being unable to speak the thoughts that cross your mind. Maybe you have something to say and yet you can't. It is very frustrating at times for Josh, but he knows he needs other people to express those ideas. He knows he isn't autonomous and relies on others, whether he really wants them around or not. That is a feat of unbelievable strength. He has humility engrained in him.

The misgiving behind a nonverbal child is that they don't have anything to say. "Quiet" doesn't mean ignorant, it simply means currently not making a sound. Sometimes, the best words to use are no words at all. Although there are many times that Joshua gets so angry that he cannot form words the way we understand them, his silence is also a gift in humility. Joshua might be misunderstood but he is never misquoted. We have trouble saying that about our own lives.

If we could stop talking, we could listen and really hear what others have to say instead of figuring out what to say next. We could be more open to helping others and understanding what they really need, becoming more selfless. Silence allows us to listen to others, to what God is saying to us. Instead, we don't revere silence. We don't like it because we don't always hear what we want to hear. We don't hear a confirmation that we're on the right path, and we don't like that. So we fill up our air with meaningless words and sentiments, trying to justify our positions in this world and, instead, end up hurting each other.

Joshua squeezed me into a more humble position in my life. Episode after episode broke down any artificial attitude that I could be someone great on my own. I was at the breaking point: confused, unsure, and unaware. Josh led me to let myself be exposed emotionally and spiritually. God invites us to come to him in that condition so that he may build us up and move us closer to where we need to be. This allowed for a newer me to become more receptive to God and the love and grace he offers. Josh showed me how needing people isn't a bad thing. After we realize there are other people we need and that we are dependent on others, it is easier to keep going. Creating that sort of dependency on God helps us to persevere.

CHAPTER 8

"You are awesome, O God, in your sanctuary; the God of Israel gives power and strength to his people. Praise be to God!" Psalm 68:35 (NIV)

PERSEVERANCE

In order to persevere, we have to keep going. We need to endure. We have to push our earthly limits. To do this, we have to have some sort of internal motivation in order to keep going.

God and my children are what drives me. He gives me strength to continue, and my children remind me daily why I keep going. Josh doesn't even allow me to question otherwise. He forces me out of bed, tired or not, and makes me get moving. He tells me without words to just keep moving. He asks me to persevere by making me wake up and do it again, even when I don't think I'm able.

It's Friday. Lyman picked up the kids for the weekend. We met halfway. I should relish this time alone, but I'm not always sure what to do with myself. I breathe deep for a moment and enjoy the silence, but only for a few minutes. Then I get nervous. I'm too tired to go out but I'm too tired to sleep. So I do the same thing every time the kids visit their dad—throw myself on the couch and stare at the wall. And here I am again, exhausted, dwindling.

My walls are blank for Joshy's sake, but they only calm me for a minute. The rest of the room, the rest of the house, the rest of my world is a mess. There are toys all over the floor amongst a carpet of dirty clothes and towels, evidence of me catching the kids wherever I can. My kitchen table is loaded with glasses, construction paper, glue, and crayons. Josh hadn't cleared that table for us. But he got to the end tables, as I can see bills, keys, pencils, and hair barrettes just below them. Josh's table is clear, save a stack of books twelve or thirteen high that I can't touch in fear of disturbing the order. I see speckles of cereal, various kinds, over here, over there, and trailing up the stairs. A mountain of dishes peek over the breakfast bar into my line of view and pour onto the adjoining counter. My vacuum is filling in as a coat rack, holding several jackets and sweaters. And I'm not sure, but my nose is betting that a dirty diaper got rolled under the couch.

I can hardly breathe. I'm tired and worn and should probably take myself upstairs to bed but I know the mess up there would only be worse. More clothes on the floor, dirty towels, and beds in need of changing. I have my work cut out for me this weekend.

I can't keep up. We dash out of the house to go to the sitter and to work. We rush home to try and eat, and before

I can even sit down to relax, it seems to be bed time. Which means I have to choose between cleaning or sleep, neither of which I do quite enough.

Much of my time with Joshua was spent simply existing. I just kept plugging along. I'd work on getting through Monday, then Tuesday, and then Wednesday, and so on. I took one day at a time. I gave Josh and the kids everything I had, trying the best I could for that day, trying to stay awake. One wrong move and a happy day could turn into a violent evening. Inadvertently, something would set Josh off, no matter how many precautions I took, and the rest of the day would be about survival rather than doing something productive. I would go to bed at night, for however long that would be, and hope for an easier time in the morning. Sometimes I would write in awe of how such a beautiful child could spin out of control at the drop of a hat.

Finally, the Tasmanian devil sleeps. Today was not so good. Evidently, he had a fit at school and was never quite right after that. He spent the rest of his day crying and bouncing on his knees, pushing anyone who came near. Anytime that he was able to calm down, trying to get him into a new activity would send him through the roof. When he's at this level, he even gets upset about dinner time.

I wonder what type of day tomorrow will be? How long can we go before our day is ruined? Once we have a fit, the rest of the day goes down the tubes. I don't have any choice but to reschedule any plans, endure until the end of the night, and pray he sleeps enough to regroup. Then we all just wake up in the morning and try again.

Raising Joshua takes persistence. There is no stopping. If I stopped, his development would be affected. He wouldn't thrive without someone there, guiding him in the right direction. Persistence is so important for Josh. Without it, there is no discipline for him, and he needs that. He needs me to be persistent in order to learn what is important in the world.

Persevering requires a persistent tenacity of spirit. The ability to endure and keep going is only the beginning. To persevere, you have to be willing to keep trying. Perseverance doesn't mean not failing, it simply means not quitting. If what you are trying isn't working, you have to be willing to do something different. After long periods of chugging through the motions, it is the ability to accept changes in plans that allow me to reconnect with my goals. Sometimes, you have to take suggestions or derive ideas from others, but you just keep moving forward, even when some of the ways you try to manage your life don't work exactly according to plan.

Soon after starting early intervention therapy, the occupational therapist mentioned that many parents saw an improvement in their child's behavior with a diet free of gluten (found in wheat flour), casein (milk protein), and lactose (milk sugar). My jaw dropped.

"So if I don't give him milk or wheat, he could get better?" I asked.

"I can't promise anything," she warned "but I have seen several kids benefit from the diet."

I thought about how hard it would be to keep bottle boy away from his milk. And how would he master the spoon without his scooping crackers? But if all of that was actually harming him, maybe this would be worth a shot.

She told me I could find many gluten-free snacks at a natural foods store. I went that weekend and almost cried when I found out how much everything cost. Gluten-free eating was expensive, and half of the items didn't even look like they tasted any good. I bought one package of animal crackers and soy milk, and went home.

Right off the bat, the animal crackers were a bust. They were horrible, and not even the boy who eats dirt would touch them. I ate one, hoping that would be the moment he would try to imitate me. I gagged. I went to plan B: rice cereal and rice cakes.

He ate the cereal for breakfast with calcium orange juice and water. Lunches were more difficult. I pushed the spoon more with the applesauce but he used his fingers. I cut up small pieces of bologna and banana. I tried the soy milk in his bottle at nap time but it was a no-go. He consequently gave up his nap for the day. Snacks were difficult. He wanted Honey Nut-Os. I hid the box in the cabinet on top of the fridge. He ate canned mandarin oranges. Dinner was hamburger and fruit. I gave him a little bit of rice cake with peanut butter. That was okay. I gave him a special animal cracker to scoop his applesauce. He threw it at me. Bedtime brought watered-down apple juice in his bottle. He was okay with this compromise.

This was his diet for the next few months. We stuck to it very closely. I hoped to see results more quickly, but I was told it could take a few weeks to see any improvement. I waited to see him be more responsive and more involved in the world around him. Maybe he would look at us more. Maybe he would try to say a few words. All the diet seemed to do was make him obsess about getting into the kitchen (a problem I still battle today) and give up his afternoon nap. Ten weeks of this therapeutic diet, and he only became more difficult to manage. I wasn't happy. Josh wasn't happy. The next time Josh charged the kitchen, I broke down and gave him Honey Nut-Os in a cup and a bottle of milk. Josh smiled at me for the first time in months. Shortly after stopping the diet, he gave up his bottle on his own accord. He never went back to his afternoon naps, though.

"Well, not everything works on every child," the therapist mentioned to me after seeing how negatively Josh responded to the diet.

I shrugged my shoulders and thought, *I don't care about other children. I just wish I could find anything that works on this child.*

Eventually, after several months of therapies, we discovered that Josh learned well through repetition. He was participating more. Rewards were okay; but when he was younger, he would fixate on them so much that he wouldn't really be learning. He was simply performing an action. If someone ran through the task holding and operating his hands (hand-over-hand instruction), he would learn each part of the activity if done multiple times. Over time, he would do the requested activity unassisted and even began to transfer the knowledge to other areas of his life. For example, instructing him on how to lift a cup to find a ball allowed him to apply it to lifting the footstool to find his pacifier. Repetition was the key ingredient to teaching Josh many skills for our world.

He was that way with spoon feeding. For every meal since he was eighteen months old, he was given a spoon. I would always have Josh try a few bites with it. As he became more tolerant of the spoon, I would fill the spoon and work on him lifting the spoon to his mouth, hand over hand. Repeatedly, we worked with a spoon at each meal until suddenly, at the age of five, he picked up the spoon, scooped his food, and fed himself.

Josh really needs that hand-over-hand teaching, steadily running through motions until he learns something. Step by step. Over and over. After that, it seems that something just clicks in his head, and the skill spontaneously appears.

I was anxious to start potty training Joshua. His sister was done and now I waited for Josh to show signs of readiness. When it came to potty training, my daughter was about as easy as they come. She was interested first. I explained what the potty chair was for, and she sat down and went. She wore big girl pants after that and only had three or four accidents from age two until five. She took one giant leap into growing up and never looked back. I knew Josh would be different but I guess I wasn't ready for how different. I had heard that potty training a child with special needs could delay the age I should start the process, but I really wasn't prepared for how long the whole process could take.

I waited until the age of three, as his early intervention therapists had suggested, and brought up the potty training subject with his teacher at school. She chuckled, said he wasn't nearly ready, that he was terrified of their school bathroom, and would always be wet at changing time. He wasn't emotionally or physically ready. So I waited.

I let a year pass. In that time, I left his father, and the kids and I moved to a new city. He switched school systems, adjusted to a different teacher, and had a new pair of therapists. I worked on introducing him to the toilet at our house, to make him less nervous about the bathroom. He was staying dry longer. His eliminating times were more consistent, so I asked again.

His teacher was glad that I was trying to get him out of diapers but she said that they were having trouble getting him to stop playing in the toilet. He had overcome his fear of the toilet by replacing it with a compulsive need to toilet dive. She reported that he would be playing with a block one minute and then dart into the bathroom and plunge into the toilet. If they had to change another student, he would run in behind them and douse himself in the toilet. Even if they were right behind him in the bathroom washing their hands, he would wriggle to the side and step into the toilet. (That answered my next question to her, about the one wet shoe.) However, even with all of his interest in the toilet, he showed no interest in sitting yet, so he probably should wait a few more months.

I was okay with that. I was having the same issues at home with Joshua and the toilet diving. He was so intense with it that I thought he was on a mission to make it the next Olympic sport. I bought a few hook-and-eye locks for the tops of my bathroom doors to reduce the amount of toilet instances. He was only in the bathroom, supervised, when we were working on sitting on the toilet.

That did not go well. For the next six months, we practiced sitting on the toilet. He hated to sit anyway, let alone with his tiny little bottom hanging into the abyss. I bought an insert so that he could sit without falling. He still hated it and would scream and hit and then jump up and try to plunge his hand into the toilet. I also tried it while he was clothed, just to get him used to the idea, but it didn't seem to make a difference and had similar results. I figured he wasn't really ready to even practice, so I waited another six months before trying it again.

A year later, he wasn't as fascinated with playing in the toilet. He was much taller at five and was more interested in faucets now. He would sit on the toilet with his pants on, for about ten seconds. Without them, he sat for less, but he was no longer afraid of falling, he just couldn't be bothered. His teacher suggested that I buy some underwear for him and let him try it. Some children with autism learn to go because feeling wet is a deterrent. I was thinking that it wasn't going to work, seeing as he didn't mind soaking his shirt sleeves in the toilet or faucets.

I was right. He would go to the bathroom while running and not even think twice about being wet or making my carpet wet. I was not sold on this. His teacher and I put it off for the year. He would be going to kindergarten next year, and we concentrated on improving his social skills to try and get him ready.

The following year, I put off asking about potty training. He had just turned six. I had started and finished toilet training Noah, and I was wondering if Josh was ever going to be any more ready. I wasn't so hopeful. The teacher approached me around Christmas time and asked if I was ready to put a plan together for Joshua's toilet training. I agreed because I really didn't want to diaper him through adulthood. I just wasn't sure what we could do.

His teacher suggested that anytime we changed his diaper, we sit him on the toilet so he could associate the whole elimination process with the toilet and work on getting him to sit longer and longer at each stretch. We kept this up for the rest of the school year, with absolutely no elimination. I wasn't even sure he understood what we were asking. We kept trying through the summer, but he was hardly interested. I even tried underwear for a few weeks. My steam cleaner earned its keep those weeks.

When we entered first grade, his teacher suggested we try schedule training. We simply take him on a schedule, and he would learn to eliminate at those times. It sounded good, but Josh did not care if he was wet, and he would not sit for very long at a time. So we decided to take him every fifteen minutes. I tried but often could only do every twenty minutes. That April, he dribbled a little, but that was the only success until that summer.

All summer, he would remove his pull-up or diaper anytime it was wet. I thought it might finally be time to make the jump to underwear. I bought more detergent for my steam cleaner and stuck Josh in underwear anytime we were at home. He would still wear a pull-up out in public, though. We started counting for his time on the toilet. I would say, "Josh. Sit for twenty," and he would wait as I counted to twenty before getting up. He learned to sit longer. We had a handful of potty successes and a zillion accidents. Anytime he was successful, he got chocolate. He either did not see the connection or he did not care.

Second grade brought with it great change. I spoke with his teacher and he wore underwear all day at school and all evening at home, using the pull-up only for night and for the bus. We were consistent in taking him every fifteen to twenty minutes. He had a handful of successes at school and was doing better at home. Then one day at school, he decided he would just go. And he kept doing it at home and then at school the next day. He finally got it.

Perseverance is being able to push through an obstacle. This can be difficult and frustrating, especially when we place arbitrary time limits on accomplishments. We are human. Undesirable things will happen. We will mess up. If we can remember that we can persevere with the expectation that we are occasionally going to go backward, it will make the journey more tolerable.

Joshua perseveres every day. It is more difficult for him to function in our world than it is for us to accept him. Even in something as simple as a trip to the store to pick up a treat for him, there are adversities. Joshua loves his chocolate, but first we must get the other few items on the list, and waiting can be difficult. There are flickering lights in bulbs that need changed, crying newborns kept out five minutes past their feedings, items he isn't allowed to have, squeaky shopping cart wheels, beeping laser scanners, people with coffee breath, and cold temperatures in the aisles. All he wants is a chocolate bar, but he must endure a total sensory assault just to be able to choose the candy that he wants. That is his world, day after day. He just keeps going.

Josh doesn't snuff out his own goals with time limits. He is tenacious until he is victorious. After thinking about how Josh keeps going and doesn't even think about stopping, I felt kind of silly. I don't really have a choice but to keep trying to make the best life I can for my kids. I've watched him closely and seen how he operates in our world. His methodical nature helped me to develop a plan of action for persevering in my life.

Have a focus for the day. Joshua always has some focus for the day. It may be to get to the swimming pool, take a bath, play outside, or get me to go to the store. He keeps trying to accomplish his "thought of the day" to the point of obsession. Sometimes, this is irritating on my end, as I feel as if I am constantly running damage control. However, in watching how he works to achieve his goal, I have to appreciate one thing: regardless of what he fixates on for the day, he sticks to it.

Watching Josh showed me how to apply perseverance in my life. Each evening, I chose a focus for the next day. Some days, it was getting to a doctor's appointment; other days, it was keeping the boys from squabbling. Whatever the focus of the day was, I would write it down and pray about it and ask for wisdom and strength to accomplish it.

Make a starter list. Although Josh doesn't have it written on paper, I get the feeling he has his own agenda of what he is going to do. It all seems to revolve around his thought of the day.

After I know what my main function is for the day, I make a list of things to accomplish for the day. The goal of this list is to keep myself focused and to not become overwhelmed. I sometimes only had one item on my list, to alleviate stress. Some days are like that. I allowed myself that freedom to go at a mellower pace on those days, and that was fine. I started slowly and worked my way up to more items at a time.

I keep my to-do list specific and reasonable; I become overwhelmed when it seems like I have too much to do. For example, I would assign myself the tasks *clean the kitchen and fold the laundry,* not *clean the house.* There were many days that there would be the same few tasks over and over again. This sometimes made me feel like I was accomplishing less, but I was doing something to move me along my day.

Just keep going. Josh just keeps trying. If I try to stand in his way of taking a bath, he tries and tries again. He's learned what things work to reach his goals and what things put him further away. As annoying as it can be sometimes, I have to admire Josh's relentless persevering spirit. So I try to do like Joshua. I keep moving, keep doing, and if I fail, I keep trying. I try to keep realistic expectations for myself. I've found out what works to keep my family and me on a forward path and what doesn't.

Josh has molded me into someone with a persevering spirit. Josh's demanding nature doesn't allow me to quit. I don't give up, even though I might restructure my path or go backward occasionally. I keep God and my family as my motivation, expecting to try and expecting to fail. I keep my patience, recognizing that all things are on God's time, even though sometimes I would like them to be faster. In raising Josh and my family, I keep going forward, making new goals and changing old ones, staying persistent no matter what.

God is persistent with us. He constantly shows up in our lives to protect us and guide us, whether we want him to be or not. He continues to love us and care for us, even when we are focusing on extraneous things. When we depend on him for strength and provision during the difficult times, he rewards our persistent spirit.

If we don't persevere, then we have resigned ourselves to failure. We will continue to stop before we accomplish anything. We give up on ourselves, our families, our dreams, and the plans that God has for us. If we are forgiving with ourselves and our time when we go backward instead of forward to a goal, then we can develop the patience it takes to persevere.

Chapter 9

"The end of a matter is better than its beginning, and patience is better than pride." Ecclesiastes 7:8 (NIV)

PATIENCE

Patience is a virtue involving the ability to wait without adverse reactions. It is also the virtue most likely to feel human. The most common response to situations requiring patience is often frustration, but if we can keep our composure, we discover that it is also the virtue most required to succeed in life.

There are times I think we are too hard on ourselves. We often have unrealistic assumptions about what we are supposed to be able to handle. To have patience means only to endure through annoyances, not to be immune to them. The difference between having patience and being impatient is a diligent perseverance. Patience is a necessary ingredient for perseverance. To keep going, we need to eliminate unproductive reactions to stressors and setbacks. Patience involves being able to quickly forgive circumstances, people, and ourselves to keep moving forward.

It is usually easier to be patient with Joshua in public. I am aware how difficult outings can be for him, and I am sensitive to what sensory problems he might be experiencing. After I am able to buffer his environment a little, I have very little control over how Joshua responds to his environment. Even in the most intimate settings, I have to accept the fact that I have only a basic say in events. I don't always know when Josh is going to melt down. The hardest time for me to have patience is in private. Behind closed doors, I don't have anyone gawking at me and watching my every move. Those staring eyes that I despise also keep me controlled. Sometimes, I become most impatient trying to teach the repetitive, mundane daily tasks.

Sometimes, it is hard to keep my cool when I am working on the same issue repeatedly. I worked on dressing with Joshua for over two years. Every day, at least twice a day (many days more because he hated wearing clothes), we worked diligently on putting on a shirt and pants. Many days, I wasn't sure he was paying attention. But if I didn't keep trying and guessing what to do next, then I was telling him I was out of answers. If I was out of answers, I was out of luck. I had to keep trying and be persistent. That seemed to be the only way he learned anything.

Slowly, Josh started to understand. First, he realized we needed his arms to put on a shirt, and he would put down objects he had been holding. He would lift his feet to put on pants, which he wasn't doing before. He later began finding arm holes in shirts after the head was done for him. He began to pull up his own pants. And eventually, at the age of six and a half, after being promised a trip to the store, he could put on his own pants and shirt.

Dressing isn't always an enjoyable task for Josh. He still isn't fond of clothes, and often he is backward or inside out, but it is rewarding to know that it pays off to keep practicing a skill. Working so closely with Joshua has made me realize how much having patience with him is a way of showing love. If he doesn't feel rushed or pressured, he is more relaxed and happier, more willing to learn and follow directions. It establishes a consistency that is conducive to trust. When someone can make him feel comfortable like that, he is able to trust them.

Josh is nonverbal. Since he entered preschool, his educational goals have centered around communication. His school therapists and teachers have spent much time and effort trying to find a way to communicate with him and to have Josh be able to express his wants and needs.

This is frustrating. Until recently, Josh refused to communicate in any way other than hand gesturing and guiding to get his point across. He refused to look at the pictures. He wasn't speaking, but other than a few common ones, he refused to use signs. He didn't like the way his hands had to move. He wouldn't even point to things. Often, he would get upset because we couldn't figure out what he wanted.

I know I get tired with this and my patience wears thin, but I couldn't help wondering about how Josh saw all of this. He would have to be a very patient person, even though it didn't appear that way on the outside. How hard would it be to wait for the right questions to be asked? It would be like playing a version of the $25,000 Pyramid where half of the team is muted. Before he used his pictures more consistently, asking for anything became an intense "conversation" between me and his body language.

Okay. I've brought her over to the fridge. She has to know I'm thirsty.

"Are you hungry? What do you want?"

Well, not really. I'll just move her hand over here and ...

"Oh, you want some ham?"

No ...

"A hot dog?"

No! Maybe if I move her arm to the other side she'll see it.

"Pasta salad?"

"*EEEEEE!*" I frustrated him enough to try to vocalize. *Here!*

"You want grapes?"

My word, woman! There! He nudges my elbow.

"What? What do you want?"

Here. If I give you this cup out of the sink, will you get it?

"Oh! You're thirsty. Do you want juice?"

Yes. Juice. I'm showing you my "more" sign now; let's get a move on with that drink.

"How about a please?"

Fine. Josh shows me the sign for "please" and puts my hand on the pitcher.

He isn't generally a very patient person. If he wants you to open a candy bar for him, he twitches, trying to wait patiently. When he was younger, he would melt down before you could even tear through the paper. Still, in some ways, he has an intangible sense of patience.

His lack of verbal skills gives him an innate gift of patience in gaining understanding. This isn't to say that he doesn't get frustrated when he can't get his point across, but there is a natural driving force to stay persistent rather than breaking down. The patience I have learned from him has come in me requiring patience to get through different situations. It is a patience that stems from being unassuming. He doesn't assume I understand, so even if he loses it, he continues until I do. Joshua thinks nothing of playing a ten-minute game of charades trying to make me guess what he wants. If I show signs that I am getting close, he is patient with me. He sees a little glimmer of hope that I might get it soon and he continues.

It seems strange. I am so tired, but I cannot sleep. Out of habit, I lay in a world half in and half out of sleep, waiting for him to move, to scream. I hear nothing; hour after hour, I dance in and out of dreams, dreams so light I hear the sounds of my room in them. I can't truly fall asleep because I never can. My body is constantly on guard as I watch Joshua sleep.

So now I am awake. The lights are dim so as not to awaken the now sleeping beast. It seems so odd. I am actually too excited to sleep. If this can happen night after night, I might actually stand a chance. Here's hoping.

Medicating Josh was my glimmer of hope. I hated the idea at first, but it was the first time that I felt that I had some sort of control over Joshua's future. I needed that glimpse of the light at the end of the tunnel. I had to gain more patience with Joshua because I had to prepare myself to learn patience with the people around him.

When Joshua was in kindergarten, I was invited to stop by his classroom during a school day so that I could see how the room was set up and what his day was like. I had told the teacher what types of things we had been working on at home—choosing colors, shapes, and letters—but Josh refused to show them even basic tasks. The teacher thought if I checked out the classroom, then maybe I could help them figure out why Josh wouldn't perform.

I took off work early one day to visit and check out Josh's work habits. I watched Josh attempt several activities, which required hand-over-hand prompting to try. They were trying to get him to identify colors with giant flash cards. They presented him with two pictures, but he would always choose the picture on the right. He did not care about trying to be correct, and he had very little attention span. I didn't see much difference in the work environments or in the way that the teacher was working with Josh, other than the fact that at home, he would answer the questions correctly. He would only sit for one or two at a time, but he would give me a glimpse of what was working in his little head.

I tried the color cards with him. Josh gave me a vacant stare and began selecting the card on the right for each answer, without even looking to see if I changed them. I was dumbfounded. This is what he had been doing at school since day one—pretending not to know anything. At home, he would try. Sometimes, he would miss, but we were still learning. At school, he wasn't even focusing on the task. I shook my head, and Josh ran off to play with a toy.

"That's all he ever does for us. We can't even get him to focus on the pictures or the cards. Are you sure he is doing this at home?" his teacher asked, trying to mask her disbelief.

"He does so much at home. He can pick out shapes from blocks, he can identify colors. He can even spell his name out on an alphabet board," I pleaded.

The teacher shook her head. "I know you've said that before, but he just won't do anything like that here. We have an alphabet board and we have tried, but he just wants to play the music over and over again."

She reached up on top of a bookshelf and pulled down an alphabet board identical to the one Joshua used at home. Josh immediately came running and took it from her. "This is the one we use for him. Does he have something else at home?"

"Not at all," I said. "It is exactly the same."

She wiggled the board away from Joshua, who was already playing the board in music mode. She handed it to me.

"Maybe you can get him to stop playing *London Bridge*."

I put the board on my lap. Josh followed and stood right in front of me, pushing the letter R to hear his song one more time. I quickly switched it to letter naming mode and placed my hand over the switch. He tried to pry my hand off of the control.

"No. Name first, then music," I said to Josh firmly.

He looked up at me and tried to lift my hand again.

"No. Type your name, then music." I pushed the J for him, hoping that he would show her. Josh ran to another part of the room.

I sighed.

"Don't be too hard on yourself. We can't force him to perform," the teacher said with a patronizing twang.

I felt as if she thought I wasn't being truthful. Josh was capable but he wasn't letting anyone else see. It was very frustrating that Josh would only learn with me. I had always been patient with Josh, but I was growing weary of educators and therapists who couldn't command the same kind of attention that I could. Josh was going to have to help me out.

"This is ridiculous," I sputtered, pulling Josh close to me as he tried to pass by.

I tugged on Josh's sleeve until he came in for a hug. He smiled.

"You know, Joshua," I whispered, "people are going to think your mom is crazy and they are going to take me away if you don't start letting them know you are a smart little guy."

He laughed at me and pushed his forehead tight against mine.

"Ha ha," I mimicked. "Very funny. Now let's try your name."

Josh giggled and jumped up and down.

"Where is the J?"

Josh quit giggling and became very serious. He focused on the alphabet board as he pushed the letters J—O—S—H on the board. He jumped up and down, laughing, as he flashed his teacher a look. He grabbed the alphabet board, ran to the other side of the room, and played the first eight notes of *London Bridge* over and over again.

The teacher and classroom aide were wide-eyed and astonished.

"So, Josh," the teacher addressed him. "What else do you know that you're not telling us?"

Josh continued to be lost in his music. I was relieved that someone else finally got to see a glimpse of what I knew Josh can do.

Josh made me be more patient with those around me. I often became defensive when it came to Joshua and his abilities. It always seemed like someone was expecting either too much or too little, and I never stopped to think why. People are always judging Joshua. Sometimes good. Sometimes badly. But they are constantly putting him in a box according to his behavior.

This happens to everyone; people normally categorize the world around them. Because many of us care about how others perceive us, we try to behave in a manner appropriate to our surroundings. We are quiet in a library and a little rowdier at a football game. We keep our clothes on in the grocery store. We don't barge into other people's houses. We show off our knowledge at school. Josh doesn't have that level of concern over what others are thinking. He really doesn't care. So his outward behavior might not match his situation or ability.

I have to keep in mind that even though people are judging him, it doesn't matter what they decide. What is important is that I am trying continuously to soothe him into the outside world. I stay patient with others, knowing that they aren't always going to see the smart, funny little man I have come to know and love. It may take time. And this is on Josh's time. He will only let people see so much at a time. Maybe it is a trust issue. Maybe it's a scam for lowered expectations. Either way, I have to realize that people aren't going to figure him out in one or two meetings. Even I am still learning to be patient with Joshua. Even though it bothers me that others try to be judgmental, surely I could give others the benefit of the doubt.

Patience is being able to tolerate and handle the things that drive you crazy. Having patience doesn't mean that things won't irritate you. Patience is more a result of reaction. It is okay to consciously discern whether an action can realistically be changed or if it is something that is just irritating to you. If you can recognize that an issue in your day, where you struggle with having patience, is something that isn't a big deal in the scheme of things, then you can focus the attention on yourself and how you can handle it.

Sometimes Josh will repeat an action or sound because he finds it comforting. Many of his behaviors result from this quest for sensory relief. When it comes to Joshua, I may have to set limits with the issue or behavior. I have to gauge how bothersome it is to his well-being. I have to be objective and decide how much it is inhibiting his development. Are others making fun of him? Is it causing a disruption at school? If it is mainly affecting me, changing my own attitudes can be easier than interrupting something that Josh might find comforting.

E flat. I hate that note. I banged on the piano until I found it. I hear it over and over again. E flat. He knows no other note. It is the note he hums for "please." It is the note he hums for "Mom." It's how he talks to his brother and sister. It is the note he hums when he is happy. It is the note I hear when he is sad. It is the note he hums as he looks at himself in the mirror or when he exhales in his sleep. I've heard it so much that it is the note that I'm starting to hum. It's a constant concerto in E flat. All E flat, all the time ...

I try to be patient with myself. I try to keep realistic expectations for myself. I try to relax and tell myself that there are going to be things about Joshua that, no matter how much I love him, drive me to insanity. To have patience is not to take yourself too seriously. Josh has forced me to alter the way I look at day-to-day life. It never fails. As soon as I start believing that I have some sort of influence over my world, Josh reminds me that he is in my world too. He refuses to be ignored and invites me to rethink my importance. I have to have patience with situations that I have minimal to no control over.

Josh reminds me that getting irritated and exasperated over certain situations does not mean I have to lose my patience. Patience involves my outward reaction to events that I can't manipulate. I can choose my response. The more patient I can be, the easier it is to move forward with my day. I remember that God has a plan for me and Joshua and can use all pieces, good or bad, to get to his final destination. I remember who is in control of the things I am not. I am able to find solace in that. The less anger I internalize, the easier patience becomes.

Patience is a perpetual process of bearing adverse events and reacting appropriately. Just when you think that you are on your way to being a patient person, something tests it. Patience comes from never assuming that life will go smoothly. When you can expect the unexpected, it allows you to keep going, even when it looks like the rest of the world is against you. Being patient is recognizing God is doing his part.

CHAPTER 10

"Every good thing given and every perfect gift is from above..." James 1:17 (NASB)

TAKING THINGS FOR GRANTED

One Wednesday evening at church, I was picking up Noah from his class. Josh had come in with me. The choir room was a classroom in the preschool wing. There was a giant calendar, posters, and colorful bulletin boards filled with artwork.

I was speaking with the children's choir director when I spotted Joshua out of the corner of my eye. He was staring at the bulletin board, wringing his hands. He was twitching, pulling his arms in closer to him.

"Joshua. Don't ..." I started to run to stop him, but I was too late.

Joshua grabbed the corner of the lime green paper and pulled it from the bottom to the top.

Joshua was laughing and smiling. It made a fabulous ripping noise and an even louder sound when he slapped the butcher paper in his hand. The choir director and I spent the next few minutes repairing the bulletin board.

Joshua always seemed to be able to make a typical stop not so typical.

Learning to not take things for granted is difficult. There are lots of things we take for granted every day: clean water, heat in the winter, a place to stay, being able to eat when we are hungry. They are things we are able to get with little effort on our part. Most of the time, they have always just been there.

I think, on average, most people realize that not everyone has a car to jump into or a meal every day and are sensitive to that, but I don't think people understand how remarkable it is to have a typically developing child. Yes, they can wear on your every nerve just like my Joshua, but as you are working with them, you don't figure that they may never learn to walk, chew with their mouth closed, or flush the toilet. You assume that they can and will…eventually. As a parent, I can't always come to that conclusion. Joshua has made me more appreciative of what we consider basic achievements.

I was thrilled when he finally started walking at twenty months. Eating off a spoon was remarkable. Being potty trained after a grueling two-year battle. Learning to buckle a seat belt. They all are normal developmental achievements, but Joshua had to work harder to accomplish them. And once they were learned, they had to be practiced repeatedly or he would lose the skill. I can't even assume that once he has learned something, he will retain it.

I think sometimes the good moments in life, even though nothing extravagant, are even more special because I can't take them for granted. For instance, when Josh started reaching for things on the store shelves from the shopping cart, I was ecstatic and would purchase the items (within reason) that he placed in the cart. That irritates most parents but I was excited he was even paying attention to the world around him. I have relished moments when Josh does things that would anger most parents.

One evening, I went to check on the uncomfortable quietness upstairs. I walked into my bedroom to see my two naked boys drawing an enormous mural on the wall by my bed. I was shocked, and my gasp scared the two boys, who were now giggling. I couldn't even get upset as I handed them both pants and a coloring book. I was thrilled that my boys, who usually ignored each other, had done something together, and I was even more excited about Joshy taking initiative to write. Previously, he had never shown interest.

It is a blessing to have to work a little harder for some of the smaller things. It is something that has drawn me closer to God. I pray more and am closer to him than I have ever been. It gives me a better understanding of others and what God wants for us to be: patient, loving, kind people helping each other. It is a blessing to raise Joshua. Blessings do not come without sacrifice. We struggle for our family time. It is harder to load the car up and go somewhere with Joshua. In turn, many of Mona's and Noah's events are done separately.

One year, Noah wanted a birthday party. He was never very vocal about such things and had never asked for one. His birthdays were usually family parties. This year, he specifically asked for a birthday party at Bounce U. So that is exactly what he got.

Noah only had a handful of people he knew to invite, so we sat down with his class list to fill the other slots. There was enough room to invite Mona and Josh as well. Noah was very excited. I, on the other hand, was nervous.

Birthday parties are supposed to be fun and joyous, and certainly so when someone else is responsible for the entertainment and cleanup. Still, my stomach churned to think that I was going to have to manage Josh in the middle of chaos. Josh had historically been terrified of going through the bounce house doors. I never understood why. He loved to jump, be it on the ground or on trampolines or on the bed. However, when he would try to go into the bounce house, he would kick and grab at the entrance.

I tried to stay positive. I kept telling myself, *He's on better meds now; he uses his headphones when things get loud,* but I couldn't stop worrying about how smoothly the party was (or was not) going to go.

"I hate birthday parties," I told my daughter. She seemed a little shocked. I tried to explain how hard these days were to put together with Josh. Mona understood right away.

The party was in the late afternoon, and the time leading up to Noah's big day was all focused on Joshua. I had to pack the goodie bags and hide them after the kids went to bed so that Josh would not steal or obsess over the candy. We had to eat at certain times so that Josh wouldn't have to have a bowel movement at the party (a long, grueling process). We had to make sure we were able to swim for a few hours right before the party so he would be calmer. We had to pack an emergency bag of snacks, change of clothes, and headphones for Josh to take to the party. We had to make sure to pick up the cake at a certain time because it was immediately after his afternoon medicine, and he would be better balanced. Picking up the cake then left a half-hour layover time before my father was picking us up for the party. I prayed he didn't undress.

Josh managed to still be clothed when Grandpa arrived to take us to the party. We loaded the car and were on our way. Josh kept in good spirits on the drive. I talked with him about what to expect. He was smiling so I thought that might be a good sign. I gave him his headphones. He put them on his ears and gazed out the window.

We arrived at Bounce U, checked in at the desk, and found our party room. Josh immediately began his frantic pacing. It happens anytime he is in a new environment, but he was still smiling at this point, so I thought we would be okay. We greeted our guests, and when everyone was there, we were led into the bounce rooms to play.

Josh walked eagerly with me into the bounce room. The inflated bouncers were open and there were no doors to enter. He quickly followed the other kids, jumping and bouncing. I wasn't even sure where Noah was. I had to track Josh. Pretty soon, I heard Josh's angry squeak. He was biting his hand and hopping on the floor. I went to remove him from the situation when Josh struck a boy who crossed his path.

I ran over to the boy and asked if he was okay. He shook his head. I think he was shocked more than anything else. I apologized and removed Josh from the room instantly. My father was waiting on the other side of the glass. He was my backup for when Josh had had enough. I knew it would happen. I just figured it would be a little longer than three minutes.

There was still fifty-seven minutes of jumping before ice cream and cake. So he left the building with Josh to take him to a park. That left nothing else for me to do but play and jump with Noah and thirteen birthday party guests and just have fun.

And we did have fun. We bounced, played basketball, and went down the slides until it was time for pizza and cake.

On our way to the party room, I began to feel guilty that I was able to enjoy myself so much without Joshua. I knew Noah needed my time, too. Then I wondered about other parents with typically developing kids. They get to do this with their kids all the time if they choose to. Do they know how precious it is?

Raising Josh has taught me to never take anything for granted. There is nothing wrong in rejoicing over small achievements. Most certainly, this is the case when it takes such effort to achieve. He has given me a better appreciation for life in general and how amazing the things we see every day really are.

Joshua has also made me place more attention on how Mona and Noah feel as siblings and to not take them for granted and to focus also on their needs. He has helped me be a better mother, a better nurturer. Even though when we began our journey, we were a little broken, he has helped us rebuild as a stronger family.

We were all excited. Josh had never shown an interest in playing in the snow before. I had tried before, and he would stand out in the snow and scream. He always hated the feel of the snow on his skin. Mona and Noah would play outside, and Josh and I would watch them through the window. In fact, that used to be the only time I was sure he wouldn't run away.

But today was different. We had ten inches of snow on the ground. Mona and Noah had been playing outside for a few minutes, and Josh was watching them like he always had. Suddenly, he began bringing me coats and hats and scarves. So he and I dressed for the snow and went outside.

So for the first time, all four of us played in the snow together. We sledded down the hill, made snow angels, and built a snowman. For the first time in a while, I was able to enjoy myself with all of my children together.

Now whenever it snows, Josh wants to play outside with everyone else.

If someone is watching our family unit, it is usually because Joshua is making a scene. This doesn't always put us in the best light. So much attention goes into the negative aspects of raising Joshua. It is a feat that takes a lot of patience, time, energy, and sacrifice. I have to wake up in the morning and push myself to keep going at times. Often, people don't get to see how much good is wrapped up in Joshua. There are so many wonderful things about him.

Joshua taught me to never take anything for granted. We tend to overlook how pure and uncomplicated life can be. We choose to make it more difficult and view things as not good enough.

I choose to cherish Josh's smiles when I can get them. I see what it means for Josh to live with passion when he is swimming at the pool, riding his bike, jumping on a trampoline, or eating chocolate. In these moments, his eyes are a mirror of true happiness; these moments are when he is just enjoying what is. Josh has taught me to hold on to the small moments and indulge in life's little miracles.

CHAPTER 11

"Whoever welcomes this little child in my name welcomes me; and whoever welcomes me welcomes the one who sent me. For he who is least among you all—he is the greatest." Luke 9:48 (NIV)

WORTH

Worth describes the value of something. We constantly seek out an item's worth. In our society, we constantly seek out how much an item will cost monetarily. Other times, we are questioning the value of something to us personally to decide if it is something we need to keep or resell or donate. Sometimes, determining worth is a matter of how much time or energy will be put into something. This process of determining worth can be rather subjective, varying from person to person.

Items hold different values for us at different times in our lives. The things that we can't live without when we are children often are discarded, sold, or placed into storage by the time we reach adulthood.

One of the first big lessons Joshua impressed upon me was the concept of worth. As soon as he decided he was walking, he became a one-man demolition team. I had to learn quickly that things are just things. Nothing more. Nothing less. Things are useful and purposeful but they are replaceable. Those items that can't be replaced are usually those things we feel let us hang on to our memories. But all of it is still just stuff.

One particular day in late May of 2008, Josh destroyed, broke, dumped, or ripped more things than any other day. It was our most financially costly day. He started early that morning on a quest for water. He wanted a bath and I ran the water for him. We had an open concept tub and vanity area that was hidden behind a wall in the master bedroom. I rounded the corner to grab some clean towels from the laundry basket. When I returned to the tub, Joshua had emptied my whole bottle of new shampoo into the bathtub to make bubbles and was grabbing the conditioner to do the same.

"Joshy!" I ran and took both bottles away from him and sat on the counter while he bathed. When he was done, I wrapped him in a towel and drained the tub. I pushed him toward his room and cleaned up the excess water.

I went to find Josh, but he was not in his room. He was in the kitchen, pulling things out of the pantry; he dumped a box of cereal and potato flakes onto the floor. I guided the dusty boy out of the kitchen and started to sweep up the mess. Joshua ran behind me and around to the refrigerator. He proceeded to pull out a pitcher of cherry Kool-Aid and tried to drink. As I was sweeping up mounds of cereal and dehydrated potatoes, a swift river of red cut across my path. He missed.

"Josh!" I screamed.

"Oooo!" he argued. He tried to run but I caught him. I took off his shirt and pants and threw them into the washing machine. I washed his face and hands and then pushed him completely clear of the kitchen.

I used a whole roll of paper towels cleaning the kitchen of the sticky spilled pitcher of Kool-Aid and the now gooey mess of potatoes and Captain Crunch. As I was finishing up, I heard a loud, tearing sound.

"Josh!" I shouted. I stood up from the kitchen floor to see Josh poised at the bookshelf, ripping the covers off my paperback books. I rushed into the living room, where Joshua sheepishly handed me the book cover he was tapping. (*Toilet Training and Autism.* I guess he thought highly of that book.) I made him help pick up his mess. He ran away after handing me five different books with more than five pieces. I had located a box to put away all of the books when I heard a scream from upstairs.

"Mom!" Mona cried desperately. "Josh is eating my doll clothes!"

I ran to her room to find Josh, still in his pull-up, on her bed, chewing happily through his second doll dress. I picked up the dress beside him and held it up to the light. It was a little wet. He was biting around the buttons and pulling them off, material and all. I turned to him and tried to grab the second dress out of his mouth. He bit down harder.

"Joshy, spit it." I pulled in small, gentle circles, trying to loosen his grip. It reminded me of playing tug-of-war with a puppy. He laughed and let go after the button popped off, along with a giant thread he snagged from the dress.

"Spit it," I repeated and held my hand out for the button. He spit it into my hand and ran to his room with a giggle.

My daughter had left her room. I shoved both dresses under her mattress in hopes that she wouldn't want them right away. I went to find Joshua to take him to the bathroom.

He was in his room, continuing his reign of terror. I caught him at his bedroom vanity, filling the inoperative sink with a tube of toothpaste. He giggled at the transparent blue stream falling into a pile.

"Joshua!" I said firmly. He threw the tube down onto the counter and shrieked.

"Potty time," I announced.

He tried to run by me, but I stopped him with my knee and edged him in the direction of the bathroom. I could tell his pull-up was dry, so I hurried with my key to unlock the door. I opened the door and forced him inside. He sat as I counted to sixty very slowly. He didn't go, so I allowed him to stand. He was pulling up his pants and washing his hands when I ran to get paper towels and glass cleaner to clean up the toothpaste.

When I returned, I found Joshua naked at the bathtub, dumping two different tubes of body wash into the running water to make bubbles.

"Joshy!" I turned off the water. "No!"

I put the pull-up on him and grabbed clothes from the closet to dress him.

"No bath," I reiterated.

I moved him toward his creation in the sink. "No, yucky. Clean up."

I showed Josh, hand-over-hand, how to scoop toothpaste into the paper towel and throw it into the trash. Josh followed. He seemed a little too excited about cleaning up the toothpaste. It seemed more of a reward than a deterrent. I thought about turning the water on in the sink to clean the mess, but I didn't want Josh to know how to turn on and off the water mains; I decided that the glass cleaner would cut the goo and clean the mirror. I sprayed, he wiped. I sprayed some more, he wiped some more.

I saw that some toothpaste had fallen to the carpet, and I reached to wipe it out of the carpet. Suddenly, I felt a cold, wet splash on my back. Josh had unscrewed the top of the bottle of glass gleaner and dumped most of it into the sink. The rest soaked my shirt.

"Josh!"

I let him run past me as I finished cleaning up the mess. I made sure the bathroom was secure and that the twenty paper towels and the empty cleaner bottle were in the trash bag before I went to change my shirt.

I hurried into my closet and grabbed the first shirt on the rack. I felt I was losing an unwinnable race against the next wave of chaos. I was right. By the time I got downstairs, Joshua was in the refrigerator. He was digging incessantly for something in the back of the fridge. He was trying to get the leftover spaghetti and, in the process, had thrown a carton of eggs onto the floor.

"Josh!" I grabbed more paper towels. "Who unlocked the fridge?"

"I did," Mona admitted. "We were hungry."

It was almost noon. I'm sure they were hungry, but they had left the refrigerator unlocked, and now there was another mess. I took the spaghetti from Josh and started to heat it.

"Oooo. Mmmmm," Josh argued.

"Clean up first, then spaghetti." I handed him a handful of towels.

Josh and I cleaned up most of the mess before the microwave was done. I put the spaghetti on a plate, grabbed a fork, and took him to the table for lunch. I finished cleaning the eggs and started making sandwiches for Mona and Noah. By the time I finished, the spaghetti was at the table, but Josh was not. I heard something like falling silverware from upstairs and ran to check out the noise.

It came from my bedroom. Josh had moved a toy box and stood on it to reach the wall-mounted DVD player. The toy box had cracked and sent Josh, a tsunami of toys, and all of the tapes and DVDs on top of the player crashing to the ground. Josh was totally unharmed and handed me a broken *Veggie Tales* DVD to play.

"I'm sorry, Josh. It's broken. It won't work."

Immediately, Josh began to throw a fit. He screamed, bit his hand, and flopped all over the floor like a trout on a fishing line. He continued for quite a while.

"I'm sorry, Josh. You need to get Mommy first." He screamed louder and then ran to his room and shut the door. He quieted down as I sorted through toys and cracked DVDs. Most of the toys weren't hurt, but the box wouldn't hold them anymore. Josh had broken two DVDs and scratched the remaining three to the point of them being distracting to watch. As I pushed the toys out of the path and took the toy box to the trash, my only thought was, *Maybe it is him or maybe it is me, but someone's meds need to be adjusted.*

My other children were watching television. After relocking the doors, I sat by them on the sofa. I hadn't seen them all day, it seemed like. Since I had gotten up in the morning, I had done nothing but cater to Josh. I spent my day fruitlessly taking him to the bathroom and cleaning up his messes. This was the first time I had gotten to sit all day, and it was nearly two o'clock. I hugged Mona and Noah and proceeded to fall asleep.

When I awoke, I began to panic. I jumped straight onto my feet and began checking doors.

"Josh!" I heard water running from the garage and opened the door. It was raining from the ceiling. There was plaster on my car and a stream of water flowing out to the door.

"Noooooooo! Josh!" I screamed while running up the stairs. Josh must have found a key and opened my bedroom. The key was swinging from the lock. I went through my bedroom and felt my feet squish into the carpet. Everything was under water in the half of the room closest to the bathtub.

I sloshed my way to the vanity, where the water was running over the counter top. I turned off the water and found a floppy Frisbee covering the drain. Josh was creating tidal waves in the brimming bathtub, slipping back and forth, back and forth.

"Joshua, stop!" I yelled so hard my throat itched. He stopped and looked at me blankly. I shook and tried not to lose it, but it didn't work.

"No! This ... no ...," I stammered in anger. I continued my babbling as I reached down and grabbed Josh's underarms and pulled him out of the tub.

I turned him around and screamed in his face, "No!"

He started his tired gaze and ran to his room, soaking wet. He slammed his door and was quiet. I scared him. This was all too much for him, and he was going to go to sleep.

I rapidly unstopped the drains in the tub and sink. I threw down every towel there was in the bathroom, and there was still water a quarter-inch deep all over. I kept trying, wringing towel after towel into the emptying tub. I saw how much water had soaked into the bedroom carpet and knew I was going to need serious help.

After using a wet vac and additional towels and squeegees, I was better able to assess the damage. I lost everything in the bathroom vanity that was absorbent or electric: make-up, bars of soap, toilet paper. The bathroom vanity was pressed wood and was already starting to warp before it dried. The carpet in the bedroom was destroyed. My dresser was slightly warped. My garage was soaked. It ruined fluorescent lighting units, children's artwork, tools, wrapping paper, and decorations. Thousands of dollars' worth in damage, all because I couldn't keep going; I couldn't make myself stay awake.

That day will go down in our family history as "the most expensive day," not only because of the fiscal amount of damage done to our wallets, but for the mental wear and tear as well. For the kids, it wasn't so bad. Other than the fact they learned their mother could holler louder than they thought, Mona and Noah seemed to see that

Mom needed help, an extra set of eyes, a wake-up call, a personal tattletale for Joshua; Mom couldn't do it alone anymore. They both learned to take more responsibility for him.

I didn't fare as well. For the first time since he was an infant, I wasn't sure my house was where he needed to stay. I worried for his safety. I obviously couldn't be on guard twenty-four hours a day. I worried for the safety of Mona and Noah. If his obsession ever turned from water to fire, we were in trouble. Once he is compelled to do something, he doesn't stop. He can't stop, and obviously I can't always stop him.

I began to question how much more I was willing to battle. What was the whole struggle worth? What was I even attempting to do? Then I calmed down and remembered one day when he had run away, how scared I was, how my mind raced, how I wondered what we would all do without him. Mona and Noah and I spent so much time focusing on including him, we wouldn't be the same without him. Josh helped us be a family. So what was I doing? I was trying to take care of Josh and keep our little family unit intact.

I always knew Joshua made an impact in my life. I worked harder, longer, to take care of him, and there was always some sort of catastrophic mess to clean up just to remind me he was there. I craved any time I could spend away from him so I could regroup and try again. Josh had made his mark in my world. I just never knew how deeply until once, when he was six, he disappeared.

School had just let out for the summer. We were a few days into break, and the kids were already acting bored.

All three kids had decided to join me in my room and pile onto my bed. I piled on top of them, trying to "crush" them. This was usually a favorite game of Joshua's, but he left quickly after the other two started shrieking and giggling. He ran across the hall to his room and shut the door.

Mona and Noah and I continued our wrestling match. We were having such fun, but then I felt a weird chill. I dropped Noah onto the bed and said, "Hey guys. Let's check on Joshy."

The door to his room was now open, and he was not there. I went downstairs and checked Mona's room and the closet. Nothing. Family room: not there. Not in either kitchen or bathroom. And as I turned, I saw the door to the garage ajar. I opened it slowly, expecting to see him standing in the flickering fluorescent light. I quickly realized that it wasn't the light flickering, but the door to the side of the garage blowing open and shut in the breeze. Josh was gone.

I didn't panic at first. Josh was always taking off, and I had always found him. I yelled to Mona and Noah that we were going to search for Josh. I left out of the side door and guessed at which hot spot Josh would visit first.

I decided to run toward the swimming pool first. I ran all around the fenced pool and pool house and saw nothing. Knowing that Josh's quests involve either food or water, I ran next to the fountain, which I figured would be his next stop since the pool house was locked. When I got there, the fountain was empty: no water, no Josh. I thought about other water sources and turned around to head to the creek.

On my way there, Mona and Noah caught up with me. We ran to the creek and followed it up and down the border of our neighborhood. Not a trace of Josh to be seen. Now nervous and out of breath, I led the kids back home, where I ran inside to call the police. I grabbed the cordless phone and went back outside to call, just in case I would see him.

I dialed the operator, who connected me with the local police department.

"Police department. How may I help you?" asked the voice on the other end of the line.

I could feel my pulse in my throat as I tried to speak. "Y-yes. I can't find my son. He … he used a broom to unlock the door and he got out. We've tried all of his favorite spots and can't find him anywhere."

"Okay, ma'am. Let me get a description of your boy."

"I'm not sure what he is wearing because I found some of his clothes in the doorway. He's autistic and can't speak."

"Hold on one second please," the dispatcher interrupted.

The pause seemed like forever. It was probably no more than five seconds but it seemed like an eternity. I was scared.

"Ma'am, is your boy about three or four?"

"No, he's six. But he is wearing a diaper. Did you find him?" I prodded excitedly. Then I felt ill. I had never given an age. They found someone, but in what condition?

"Ma'am? You say he's six. Hold on please."

I grew sicker. I could feel my stomach churning and hoped the police hadn't found anyone that was struck by a car or drowned.

"Ma'am, I'm on the radio with an officer who believes he may have your son. You say he won't talk?"

"That's right. He is autistic." Something in the tone of the dispatcher's voice made me believe that he was alive.

I heard her relaying the information to someone else. I heard a garbled voice replying.

"Okay, ma'am? They have stopped your son at the corner of 86th and Crooked Creek Road. Do you need a car to pick you up?"

"No, I'll be right there," I replied and hung up the phone. I recruited a neighbor to stay with Mona and Noah. I was ecstatic. Instead of hopping in my car, I ran. They found him less than a quarter-mile away, but after circling the neighborhood a few times, my legs were burning. I didn't stop though.

I ran until I came upon a portion of the road with cars parked along both sides of the busy street. On the opposite side of the road from where I stopped, there was a crowd of people around the drainage ditch in the front lawn of a house. I had trouble crossing until a police officer saw me and stopped traffic to let me in.

I ran across the street and through the crowd of people into the center of their circle. There was Joshua, sitting with a woman on her lawn, who was trying to keep him still.

"Oh, Joshua!" I ran and scooped him into my arms. I held him tightly as he smiled and giggled.

"Thank you, thank you," I said as I turned and saw how many people were out in the yard with my son. There were a dozen people at the scene, each doing their part to keep Joshua in the grass instead of running away. A dozen strangers felt that Joshua was worth stopping their day. It gave me hope.

One of the hardest issues I face in raising Joshua involves worth. It is hard for me to look at Josh and realize that not everyone will love or revere him the way that I do. There are a special handful who do, but most peacefully tolerate him. And there are many people in this world who feel his worth to society in general is very low. They see him as a burden or something to overcome rather than a blessing in disguise.

In a conversation with a neighbor, she brought up my life. She saw daily how consuming life with Josh could be. It seemed to pain her that I was a single mom with three young kids.

"It's not fair that you are on your own with these three kids and that Josh is the way he is." Her inflection made it sound like a tragedy.

I was still dumbfounded and trying to figure out how to respond when she asked, "So what is his prognosis?"

I hate this question. I understand it, but I hate it. I guess it bothers me because it usually comes from people who don't understand Josh in the first place. It's a question that goes beyond typical curiosity. Its words suggest to me that the person with whom I am speaking thinks of my son as a disease rather than a gift.

I don't remember how I answered her. I probably gave her my usual spiel about finding Josh's vocational niche and getting him into a group when he is a young twentysomething.

I'm sure I smiled politely and nodded my head a lot, trying to be cordial and not loosen my tongue. I do recall leaving her porch thinking, "Is that really how she sees my Joshua?"

No. That wasn't how she viewed my son. As I got to know my neighbor better, I learned that our first conversation and her true opinion did not match. She watched with excitement as Josh grew, learned to ride his bike, and got better in how he responded to people. She cares for him and is amazed at how our family works. She never intended to say anything disparaging to me. My neighbor would never want me to feel that that was her opinion.

That may not be the person's intent, but words are important. He isn't his diagnosis. Josh is a little boy with autism. Josh is my little boy. His autism is just one of the challenges that he (and those around him) have to embrace. Unfortunately, for every caring and supportive person I meet, there are at least ten who aren't so warm and receptive.

Josh is a difficult person to eat with during a meal. He needs constant attention to use a fork, and it doesn't come naturally for him. He prefers his hands over utensils. And to top it off, he has swallowing issues. No matter what size the bite, about 20 percent of it comes back out. When he is done, there is always a half circle of scraps around his high chair and a shirt that is covered with food.

I know it isn't pretty. I am always a little embarrassed when we go out. I even understand looks of disgust; what I have a problem with is when those looks turn to disdain.

I think in general people try to be tolerant, but they really don't understand what it means to be accepting of someone with autism. I think it's a matter of what we are taught to believe.

Every day, I face those things that Josh is often oblivious to: the teasing, the laughing, the pointing. Sometimes, when he is babbling, squeaking, wearing his headphones, or paper slapping, he becomes a very blatant target. Even parents who are well intended refuse to correct their children when they tease someone with autism or another disability. There are always comments parents pretend not to hear. Ignoring the situation tells the children that this is okay and perpetuates children and adults with special needs as acceptable outlets for teasing.

God bless America. It is still a land of opportunity, and I wouldn't want to live anywhere else in the world. Unfortunately, we live in a society that places a lot of emphasis on occupation and vocation. It is these things that gain us resources and material wealth. Neither of these are bad, but we tend to use them as a social focal point to determine someone's place in society.

"What do you do [for a living]?" we ask people we meet, total strangers, solely as a topic of conversation. We use it to find common ground or interests for conversations to form friendships. When someone asks, "What do you do?" there is more being asked than just the question.

Joshua can't answer the question. So what does someone who uses these questions to get to know, "feel out," or judge someone decide about Joshua? Is this someone I want to know, be like, or have as a friend? Many reduce his perceived worth in their eyes. We have been inadvertently conditioned to use the answer to this small question to compare and make judgments on whether or nor we want to have another encounter. We don't even consciously know we are doing it. So, what does Joshua do?

I've pondered this a lot. Since he can't speak for himself, I wrote what he might say if he could respond to "What do you do?"

I can run and swim and ride my bike. I am fast like the wind.

I am a patient. Every doctor I see becomes a little less quick to judge.

I am a student. I can learn and grow. Over time, I can figure out your world.

I am a son and a brother. I may not want to play, but I can smile and laugh when I see you are near.

I am love. I can't say the words you want to hear, but I can show you love without limits through good and bad.

I am a teacher. I can lecture on life without opening my mouth.

I am a child. I laugh. I cry. I hurt. My chest tightens when someone laughs at me.

I am a person.

God wants us to revere everyone in the same manner. The richest men on earth are to be no more important than Steve, who lives behind a dumpster on Main Street. We don't always do that. People with autism may be tolerated, but they aren't always respected or given the compassion that they need to be successful in our world. We can teach people how to act with a learned compassion to everyone. Anything that is learned and practiced can become natural.

However, worth is evaluated in tune with our priorities. What we value mirrors what our priorities are in life. How we are with our things is reflective of our personality. We can only have compassion for others when we see the well-being of others as more important than our things, more important than our status. When we start viewing people as more important than things, then material worth is diminished and the value placed on ourselves and others increases.

God intended for us to be compassionate to others. God has a purpose for every creature he put on this planet. I know that Joshua is the way he is for a reason. Maybe it is simply to keep me busy. Maybe it's for enlightenment or another piece in a grand plan that I don't know about. Josh has made a big impact in other people's lives as well.

Josh and I decided to go to the pool. Josh really wanted to go. Mona and Noah were with my mother, and I was in between jobs so we had a few hours to kill. We changed into our swimsuits and off we went.

Once we entered the pool, Josh kept running over to the far fence. Each time, he would touch the fence and then the ground, three times. I would call his name, and he would head toward the stairs, stop, and run for the fence again, laughing and tapping the ground. He did this several times and refused to get in the water. I walked to the fence to see what was happening.

Josh was jumping happily and slapping the ground. I looked at the cement and saw something glimmer. It was a gold cross necklace with a date engraved on the back. Josh looked intently at the necklace in my hand and then quickly ran to the pool stairs to get in the water.

He had been trying to let me know that he found something. I put up found signs later at the pool. I got a call the next day from a woman whose husband had lost the baptismal cross his church had given him as an infant. She described the cross to me and told me what date was inscribed on the back. I took the cross to her house and she gave me a reward.

I had only spoken to the wife that day. About four years later, the husband approached me at the pool, thanking me again and telling me how important the cross was to him. He wanted to do something to repay Josh for finding the cross. I told him that wasn't necessary.

Then he said, "If it wasn't for him, I wouldn't have it today."

That made me think. I would never have found the necklace on my own. It wasn't near where I had set our towels. But because Josh was preoccupied with shiny things, he was able to find it on the ground. If Josh wasn't there, his cross may have slipped into the grass or been stepped on and broken.

Everyone is worthy of compassion, of love, of respect. Josh lives in a world that he is struggling to fit into. In many parts, he spends his time having to prove himself worthy to be given basic respect and treated like other kids. Sometimes, he finds it hard to find even an honest tolerance of his true self. Josh may not understand social constructs or how to hold a conversation, but he does feel when someone is taunting or laughing at him. It hurts him, just like it would any other boy his age. Joshua doesn't necessarily want to be included in everything that his siblings or peers do, he just wants to be accepted for who he is and celebrated for what he can do.

Josh has shown me firsthand that no one's worth is bigger or smaller in God's eyes. We are all his creations, and he loves us the same. There will always be people who feel you are less than they are or incapable or inadequate. Regardless of how others describe us, we shine in his eyes.

Joshua has taught me about how it is important to put others above ourselves. We need to be compassionate to and understanding of everyone regardless of what they are able (or unable) to do. Taking care of Josh prepared me to see that regarding others more highly still wasn't an excuse to neglect myself. I needed to hold myself in a higher regard as well. Even though I put others first, I couldn't take care of anyone if I was overtired or hungry. I needed to be better to others and me. If I think nothing of myself, then I can't take care of my kids or keep up with Josh's antics.

Joshua definitely keeps me busy. He is an unpredictable whirlwind of activity that keeps me on my toes. People frequently ask me how on earth I can spend time with my other son and daughter and still be able to care for Joshua. It isn't easy. There are many days I want to beat my head on a wall, but I love my children. They are all blessings; and it is because I have internalized the idea that Josh is such a blessing in my life that I can see that I don't *have* to take care of Joshua, I *get* to take care of Joshua. And that opportunity, next to having my children, has been one of the greatest gifts that I have ever received.

CHAPTER 12

"Do nothing from selfishness or empty conceit, but with humility of mind and regard one another as more important than yourself." Philippians 2:3 (NASB)

UNCONDITIONAL LOVE

Everyone desires unconditional love. Who wouldn't want to be loved constantly without stipulation or regulation? I think most of us as parents would hope we could answer honestly that this is how we love our children. But it wasn't until Joshua that I realized what "unconditional" really meant.

Sometimes, children with autism have trouble showing affection. This was true with Josh as a newborn. He really didn't want to be touched. When Josh arrived home from the hospital, he wore a heart monitor that alerted us if his heart rate went out of range. The box looked like a cable receiver with wires that extended from the monitor to his chest. There was a battery option, but for the most part, Josh remained within a six-foot radius of the outlet. This made holding him difficult and awkward and also made chasing a one-year-old nearly impossible. He preferred that I just left him alone, and he would cry when I would pick him up for a feeding. So often, I would just play with my daughter and stay within eyesight of the baby. The monitor was doing nothing for the bonding process. I felt more and more detached from him every day.

After a couple of months of what was thought to be colic and rapid growth, the monitor was going off nearly five or six times an hour. The pediatrician had to reset the levels on almost a weekly basis, and even then, it would sound an alarm for a happy, breathing baby. I felt like I was pushing a snooze button every time I reset the monitor.

Finally, after one "scare" too many, I called the company to pick up the heart monitor. I couldn't bond with my alarm baby. It had been two and a half months, and I really didn't know much about this child other than he could scream and his respiratory system was strong.

The company refused. I even told them that I wasn't planning on paying for any services beyond today's date. They wouldn't pick it up without the ordering doctor canceling the script.

So I called the pediatrician. I sent out my plea and told her my dilemma. She reluctantly revoked the script and told me that it was against her best judgment and if anything happened before the original order had expired, that I would be charged with negligence and that I could lose my daughter as well. I was still adamant.

With the machine gone, I was more nervous. I carried him everywhere to make sure he was safe. Josh wasn't thrilled with this at first, but he got used to me holding him. I was able to bond with the former alarm baby and feel comfortable in learning to love my baby even though he mostly wanted to be left alone at the beginning. I was able to desensitize him to being touched. He even learned to favor being held over sitting in his seat.

Josh has grown so much from the baby who wanted nothing to do with other people. He is often overly affectionate now. The problem is that this affection isn't always out of love. The hugs and kisses are usually in an effort to get something. "I want juice, so you get a kiss." His true attachments to people are hard to come by.

Often, when Josh craves hugs, he actually has some sort of sensory need. It isn't so much that he loves who he is hugging, it is that his body is in need of pressure and he would take hugs from just about anyone at that point. The same goes for Josh needing to feel water on his skin. It fulfills a similar sensory need.

Josh really enjoys the feel of water; he wasn't even picky about where it came from. Faucets, puddles, pools, washing machines. Reaching a water source was always the goal of the day. He always tried to play in the toilets when he was younger. I used to say he was going to make toilet diving the next Olympic sport. He just can't help himself. Water is one of his compulsions.

One day, he got into the downstairs bathroom and climbed onto the counter. I had secured all the locks before I went upstairs to fold laundry. Somehow, he found a key and let himself in. He turned on the water and plugged the sink.

I finished folding the laundry and came back downstairs. From the stairs, I could hear the faucet. I knew before I got to him what was going on. "Josh!"

My feet hit the squishy rug in the living room. I froze. The kitchen was at least an inch underwater, and as I turned to the bathroom, I found a squealing boy in the sink, laughing. I lunged for the faucet and turned off the water.

The water flowed over the counter like a waterfall as Josh spun himself off the counter. He was thrilled with his new wading pool. He jumped up and down, slapping the floor and splashing my legs.

"Joshua! Go upstairs!" I screamed.

"Oooooo." He tried to argue as I nudged him through the doorway.

My feet stood in a few inches of water; the cabinets were open and the contents under the sink were wet and ruined. The hair accessories were salvageable, but the toilet paper was not. Three boxes of tissue stacked in the back and a box of tampons were candidates for the garbage. I started grabbing towels to dam up some of the water. And out of desperation, I used my steam cleaner as a wet vac. (DON'T do it. It is NOT recommended, as it goes against the manufacturer's instructions.)

I cried and screamed, spending the next forty minutes emptying the steam cleaner and drying corners and cabinets. When I was finished, I positioned a fan to blow on the floor and under the sink. I leaned on the wall, examining my bathroom. The fan was whirring a long E flat. I slinked down the wall and fell into a fetal position, weeping.

Unconditional love does not exclude exasperation. Loving unconditionally does not mean that you will not get angry or that you are always agreeable to everything a person says or does. Frustration in a relationship is a two-way street, whether the relationship is between two friends, siblings, a husband and wife, or a parent and child. Joshua has had many occasions where I have pushed him into doing something he did not want to do. I have had many times I didn't want to be in situations where Josh put me.

However, loving an exceptional child means loving them when no one else may, staying patient when no one else will, and being forgiving when no one else can. Unconditional love involves being understanding when others are quicker to judge. I always try to keep a good sense of humor to encourage a forgiving spirit.

Forgiveness is a huge component in loving unconditionally. To love unconditionally and continually, you have to be able to be forgiving. Sometimes, it involves needing to forgive multiple times. Josh flooded that same area again after that day. He did it three times over the course of a month, in fact. Although I go back to a bathroom schedule following those incidents rather than allowing him free bathroom access, I forgive him each time.

Josh is forgiving with me as well. I get frustrated and lose my cool. I am human. He seems to understand when I apologize and gives me smiles and kisses. Josh loves me unconditionally, too. He is even forgiving when I know he isn't going to like what happens next, like when it comes to doctor's visits.

Josh has never been very cooperative when it comes to seeing the doctor or the dentist. Every visit involves some sort of restraint to check the ears and eyes, get vitals, give shots, or clean teeth. I guess this is to be expected, but somehow, I am always the one who has to be involved in the restraining process. I guess it doesn't matter that I am paying the doctor or hospital to take care of my son. Somehow, I am always strongly encouraged to participate.

Once when he was three, Joshua swallowed a mushroom at a park. I had caught him playing in a patch but didn't think he had ingested anything. I had checked his mouth and there was nothing. There were no scraps on his lips, mouth, shirt, or hands. I thought I had pulled him out of the grass in time.

Later that evening, he started vomiting and had diarrhea. I found little chunks of mushroom in his diaper. I left Mona and Noah with my parents and went to the emergency room.

The first thing they wanted to do was run an IV so they could rehydrate him and run some blood tests to check for toxins. Even though he was dehydrating and only a tot, it took three people to run the IV: one nurse to find the vein, one to hold his lower body from twisting, and me laying on the gurney holding his head, arm, and torso still against my body. Who is the bad guy in that story?

I felt horrible, but Josh still wanted me to hold him after it was over.

That is pretty much how every doctor visit has gone from checkups and vaccines to dental visits to MRIs or other tests. But every time, he forgives me. He seems to understand ultimately that I am trying to help him and not hurt him. He knows that I love him and he forgives me.

When he was younger, my love wasn't always reciprocated. I wasn't even sure he loved me at all. At the age of four, Josh would spend a lot of time sitting in front of the window, playing by himself. He didn't want to be bothered unless it was time to eat. He just wanted to be left alone.

I watch Josh playing with his pegs in the window. He concentrates on sorting them, spinning them. He sits in the sill of a giant bay window but plays completely unaware of the world on the other side. All the trees, squirrels, cars, and people, he pays them no mind. He doesn't notice anything in that window. He just keeps to himself and his pegs.

He doesn't see my reflection in the side glass or that I am standing right behind him. Many days I feel that I might as well be on the other side of the glass, an outsider looking into Josh's world.

He will never see how much I love him. He can't even see me in the room. He doesn't know how much I had to change in my life to love him. I changed the ways I knew how to love and how far I would let myself love. I learned to love without limits and without expectation.

I'm not sure what this ride has in store for me. I'm not sure what I have to do to reach Joshua. One minute I think we are making progress, and the next we are further behind. I'm not even sure what we are supposed to be accomplishing with Joshua. I can't even break through that blank stare sometimes.

But I'm realizing that the world's expectations for Joshua are on the outside of that glass. Joshua won't see them out there with the leaves and the grass. Maybe that's where I should leave them, too. I am on this side of his glass.

Sometimes, I feel like a tool. I am only a way for him to get what he wants. Even when he does pay attention to me, it's not really because I am me. He may not want to spend time with Mom just to show me love. He may not always see me, but I am here.

I am the one who loves him no matter what happens on the other side of that glass. I love him when he has had a good day. I love him when his day hasn't gone so well. I love him when the rest of the world cannot. I love him through anger and sadness. I love him when he smiles. I love him when he makes me smile. I love him when he makes me cry. I even love him when he drives me crazy. Things are different from what I thought having a son would be like, but I love him for who he is. He knows no other way to be other than genuine. I love him for just being Joshua.

Does Joshua love me? I would hope so. I love him more than he will ever understand. And once in a while, I see a little bit beyond those eyes when I'm giving squeezes and I think he really does love me. Then he goes for the ham …

Joshua is a magnificent blessing to our family. Mona, Noah, and I have learned so much about patience, understanding, and love. However, blessings do not come without sacrifice. Our family has made many sacrifices in our world out of love for Joshua. We have locks on all of the rooms and bathrooms. We limit our houseguests to a handful of familiar people. We have to plan events as a family rather than having any spontaneity or flexibility.

Many of these sacrifices would seem burdensome to the outside eye, but we do it to keep Joshua safe and comfortable. We do it out of love.

Being able to internalize and learn how to love unconditionally can make many other things in life easier. We can grow in patience and understanding when we learn how to love unconditionally. The key is to love others more than ourselves. Truly loving unconditionally involves loving and serving, even if it isn't obvious that you are loved in return; it is the same type of love God gives to us every day. It is the way God wants us to love others. Unconditional love is a mix of sacrifice, perseverance, and forgiveness, causing you to be able to love someone no matter what.

CHAPTER 13

"Do not judge, and you will not be judged. Do not condemn, and you will not be condemned. Forgive, and you will be forgiven." Luke 6:37 (NIV)

FORGIVENESS

Forgiveness is being able to accept an apology from someone who has wronged you and then (now here comes the clincher!) being able to let it go.

No one is perfect. If you have spent longer than a year on this planet, you have surely made a mistake. Maybe you broke or stained something belonging to someone else, or maybe you hurt them in some way. Forgiveness is needed for both the giver and receiver, whether the action was accidental or purposeful. If you aren't given that opportunity to try again, a fresh start, then it is easier to dwell on our mistakes than grow in a more perfect manner. If you are refusing to forgive, you are choosing anger over love and causing yourself unnecessary physical and mental strain. Through forgiveness, we are able to grow and move past negative things in our life.

Forgiveness is a cyclical concept. Each piece is just as important and necessary as the next. It doesn't really matter at which point the cycle is started, as long as it starts somewhere. We must forgive others, forgive ourselves, ask for forgiveness, and be forgiven.

One long, rainy Thursday, the kids and I returned from school. It had been a long day at work for me, extremely busy and physical. As usual, everyone wanted to eat. I told everyone to wait until I used the restroom. When I returned to the kitchen just three minutes later, it was total chaos. Everyone was foraging through the fridge to find a snack. Noah spilled the milk as he was pouring it, Mona had a foot-long sugar trail from the sugar bowl to her cereal, and Josh had his hand in a jar of peanut butter.

I made the other two clean their messes, and I led Josh to the sink to wash his hands. (For a boy who loves water so much, he hates to wash his hands.) He was getting unnerved because I was cleaning him up. When we were done, I scooped a little peanut butter into a bowl with a baby spoon and pointed him toward the table. I cleaned peanut butter and sugar remnants off the counters and cabinets. I heard Mona yell, "Josh!"

I went toward the table. Josh had his hand in Mona's bowl. Milk and cereal were dripping onto the floor. I ran over with a towel and cleaning spray. Mona and Noah took their dishes to the sink and went upstairs. I continued to clean. When I was through, I looked for Josh. He was now sitting on the couch with a straw in a bottle of Italian salad dressing, sipping it like a soda.

"Oh, Joshy!" I said, exasperated. He hastily handed me the dressing, spilling some of it on the cushion, and then darted upstairs. I wiped the dressing off the couch, remembering why I had purchased the pleather couch in the first place. I threw my cleaning rag in the washing machine and poured myself a glass of iced tea.

Suddenly, I heard the sound of water running. I put the child lock on the fridge, set down my tea, and ran upstairs. Josh had gotten into the master bathroom, which is always locked. He found my car keys and used the house key to unlock the door. I walked into the bathroom to find Josh trying to make a bubble bath with an entire bottle of shampoo, two tubes of body wash, and a little jar of scented body cream. Most of it hit the tub, but there were long streams of soap on the walls and floor near the bathtub.

"Joshy, no. It is time to play," I said, handing him a few cars from the bedroom floor and redressing him. "We'll take a bath tonight. It's play time, now." I got him interested in his cars and then wiped the soap and cream off the floors and walls. I left the rest in the tub because he could use it to bathe later. I locked the door behind me and took my keys. Josh had left the cars and the bedroom.

I heard cabinets banging in the kitchen. I ran downstairs.

"Mom! Joshy's eating vitamins!"

I rushed over to him, trying to be calm. "Uh, oh. These are vitamins. You had your vitamins today." I took the jar away from him. He had two in his mouth.

I remembered how many vitamins I used to eat as a kid and figured he would be fine. I scooted him out of the kitchen. I took the jar and placed it back into the cabinet. I noticed that he had filled my iced tea with about fifty of my herbal supplements. (I always put his medicine in his juice.) I dumped the iced tea down the sink. Making a mental note that he was now able to push down and turn, I went to the garage to fetch another child lock.

As I was putting the lock around the cabinet handles, Josh sped around the corner. He was in the garage, searching the canned food pantry. He stood there, signing "more."

"What do you want?" I asked, sighing heavily.

He handed me a can of pears, and we went back to the kitchen. I opened the can, drained the pears, and gave him a bowl and fork to take to the table. I deadbolted the door to the garage and checked the locks on the pantry and refrigerator (they often get undone by the other two children). I went to the couch to sit and realized Josh wasn't at the table and neither was his bowl, but the fork was.

"Mom!" Mona yelled. "He's got pears in my bed!" I ran back upstairs. Josh had attempted to eat his pears in his sister's bed, lying down and cozy. Instead, the pears and juice had dumped out of the bowl, and he was eating them off of the sheets.

"Josh!" I was growing more aggravated. We had been home for forty-five minutes, and I had not yet been able to sit. Josh quickly scooped the last few pears into his hand. He ran to his room and shut the door.

Mona helped me strip the bed. The juice from the pears had soaked through to the mattress. I asked Mona to get me the cleaning spray and a new towel. She returned with both items, and I scrubbed her mattress. She went downstairs to do her homework. I followed her shortly with the pile of sheets and covers from her bed. I threw them into the washing machine and started the wash.

It was time to take Josh to the bathroom. I was hoping he hadn't already gone. I walked back upstairs and opened his door. No such luck. There was Josh at his mirror, shrieking and giggling, in a shirt that was soaking wet. He had removed his pants. The carpet by the mirror was wet as well, and to make matters worse, he had pooped in the corner and attempted to wipe his backside with his pillow. I wanted to cry.

I made him pick up his mess and throw it in the toilet. Then I made him sit.

"This is where we poop," I said firmly. "We use the potty." He sat for a few minutes, and then I let him get up and flush. He was dirty, but I wasn't about to reward him with a bath. I removed his shirt and coaxed him into the tub. I proceeded to turn on a cool shower so he might understand that this was not fun time.

I cleaned him off with a washcloth and lots of soap and then wrapped him in a towel. I walked him to his bed, threw the pillow into a trash bag, and went downstairs to set up the steam cleaner. He stayed there until he saw me return with the carpet cleaner. When I turned it on, he ran naked out of the room. I wanted to finish the carpet before it soaked in too far. About ten minutes later, I was done. I grabbed underwear and some sweats and went to look for Josh.

Mona and Noah were watching television downstairs. I found Josh back in my room, destroying my books:

flipping them up in the air, tearing out pages, and slapping the book jackets. I had taken great pains to hide them away in a drawer to keep them out of harm's way. I lost it.

"Joshua!" I screamed at full volume. My voice echoed on the bare walls. "I have had quite enough!"

I ran toward him, grabbed his arm, and pulled him to his feet. I pointed to the torn book remnants.

"No. We do not tear Mommy's books." He gave me a goofy smile that sent me over the edge. I gave him a swift swat on the rear end.

"No. Not funny! Time-out!" I lifted the now crying Josh under the arms and held him straight out in front of me. I dumped him in his room, shut the door, and turned to clean up the mess. Joshua opened the door and tried to follow me.

I picked him up again and moved him farther back into his room. "You are in time-out! You need to calm down!"

He crawled into the bed, crying, and put his pillow over his head. I rushed out of the room and slammed the door. I went to my room. Instead of attending to the mess, I lay down on my bed and put a pillow over my head.

I lay there for a while. Both Noah and Mona visited me to see what was going on and then continued playing. I felt awful.

Josh had always been a hyperactive child. I know that his mind hops from one impulsive thought to another. I get frustrated because raising Josh is like raising a four-foot-tall toddler. He has the mind and impulsivity of a two-and-one-half-year-old, but the physical competence of a child of seven. I know I need to try harder to keep on an even keel, because when I yell, we only move backward and it slows his learning. I wondered how much progress I ruined with the day's episode. I felt depraved.

"God forgive me," I whispered a prayer. "Give me the strength and energy to handle Josh when he gets like this." I stayed under the pillow for a little while longer. I took a deep breath and reminded myself that I am only human. I promised myself that I would try harder. I got up to check on Joshua.

He was still in his room on his brother's bed. His head was on top of the pillow and he was snuggled in the covers. I walked over to the bedside quietly and sat on the floor. Slowly, I inched closer until I was able to rest my chin on the mattress and look into his big brown eyes.

He was sad and distant. He was sucking on his tongue like he did when he was a baby and would lose his pacifier. I gently stroked his forehead.

"Hey, guy," I said softly. "I'm sorry I got so upset. I shouldn't have screamed at you or given you a spank. I didn't want to hurt you, I just needed for you to stop and calm down. I'll work on that. Can you forgive me?"

His eyes were looking at me now. I got up on the bed and lay next to him. I dried his eyes with my sleeve and gave him a kiss on the forehead. He put his arms around me and hugged me. He chuckled and smiled.

"I love you, too, Bud." I hugged him right back.

Forgiving Others

Joshua has a beautifully primitive way of forgiving. He seems innately to understand overreaction and is willing to accept a sincere apology. He is a perfect example of the child-like faith and heart we need to have to forgive completely. If Joshua doesn't feel that fullness in an apology or there is a lack of one, he becomes the poster child for what can happen when we are unable to forgive. It consumes us.

Swimming is one of Josh's favorite activities, and once he was able to swim well unassisted, it became one of my favorite activities, too. Just a few short years ago, I would have to be prepared to sprint after him at a moment's notice. Now, it's more relaxing. He will actually stay at the pool. It is such a relief to feel a little normalcy in our lives. While Josh and his siblings swim, I am able to watch them and actually socialize with my neighbors.

One afternoon while swimming on a cool day, I sat outside the pool talking with a neighbor couple. Their children were of similar ages, and our kids were playing together in the pool. Lying near us was a young man about mid-twenties who was sunbathing. The couple and I were talking about schools and kids' sports when Joshua got out of the water and approached me.

He signed to me, "Eat please." I reached into the pool bag and pulled out a package of fruit snacks. I held them just out of reach. He smiled and gave me a kiss as he snatched the fruit snacks and ran to sit on the cement bench. He sat quietly eating and swinging his legs, slapping his hand on it every few swings. He loved that bench. He would press on it for hours if I'd let him. Probably something to do with a sensory need.

The pool often brought out a lot of odd behaviors for Josh, and the odd behaviors usually brought on a host of questions directed to me about him. This day was no different. Josh excitedly let out a roar and jumped to his feet, slapping and pressing the bench with two hands. The noise scared the kids in the pool. The sunbather shifted to a seated position and opened his briefcase. I shook my head and sighed.

"So …," the neighbor lady started politely.

"Autism," I anticipated. "He really likes that bench." Josh continued jumping and slapping and giggling.

I answered the couple's questions as they came. How old is he? Where does he go to school? Nothing out of the ordinary. I tried to explain his sensory needs and why he has certain quirks as we watched him pace back and forth, back and forth. He fixated on something and stood uncomfortably still. All of a sudden, he darted toward the sunbather, reached across the lounge, and stole the paper on which he was writing.

The sunbather yelled directly at him, "What the @#&!?" Josh was stunned. He handed the paper back to the sunbather and stared at him, confused. The neighbor couple turned away, shocked. I was stunned, embarrassed, and angry all at the same time.

"I am so sorry," I said to the man as I gently pulled Josh out of his way. The man said nothing. He just went right back to writing.

Josh was hurt. He kept looking at the man, as if he was waiting for some sort of response. But there was nothing. I gave Josh a hug and encouraged him to get back into the water.

Conversation with the neighbor couple dwindled after that. They soon collected their children and left. We followed a few minutes later. Before we left the pool house, Joshua raced back to the cement bench by the man and hit it as hard as he could, letting out a gigantic

"Aaaagggggghhh!" He immediately walked back to the door and went home. Josh was mad.

I couldn't blame him. I was upset as well. I know it had to be a terrific shock to the sunbathing man to have his paper fly away in midsentence. If you don't know life with Josh, you really aren't prepared for that. I get that. I could even understand letting something that hideous slip out of your mouth accidentally, but to not apologize for yelling a curse word at a mentally challenged child at a pool with school-age children, that is just awful. If it had not been for the other neighbors I was talking to, I may have said something unsavory to him.

That wouldn't have been right either. It took me quite a while to forgive him and let it go. It hurt me to know there are people out there willing to treat people with special needs this way. Not everyone is going to love Josh, but he deserves the basic respect that all human beings need. I boiled for about two and a half weeks before I could get a grip. I never confronted the sunbather. It was one sided, and he would never acknowledge, let alone apologize for, his behavior. I had to accept that.

Josh, however, could not let it go. Josh understands that people get angry. Josh understands that people make mistakes. Josh forgives me when I get unnecessarily upset because I tell him that I am sorry. He never heard a sorry from our tanning neighbor, and he wasn't going to let it rest.

After that, whenever we were at the pool at the same time, Josh would purposely pace closer and closer to his chair. He'd suck up pool water in his mouth and try to spit it at the man. He would try to steal his food when he slept. When we would get to the pool before him,

Josh would put his towel in the chair that the sunbather always favored. He checked on the pool constantly from his bedroom window. Josh would get irritated if the man was at the pool and scream out his war whoop. Aaaagggghh! The sunbather would never say anything. It was a summer-long grudge match.

Sometimes, forgiving others can be difficult, as the people who hurt us may not know they did anything or don't always care to seek our forgiveness. Even without their permission, we can still forgive them. We can let go of the anger and negativity that they left when we were wronged. The only thing that a wrongdoer can force on you is the original wrong; after that, the anger, resentment, mistrust, and supernatural bereavement is what you are doing to yourself. Even in the most extreme circumstances, forgiveness is possible. They don't have to ask us for forgiveness so that we can move on with our lives, we only have to forgive them.

We as humans typically give conditional forgiveness. We can forgive people as long as they don't wrong us again. When they do, we revoke that original forgiveness and become upset at two different events at the same time. This is self-defeating. Not only has the second issue not been resolved, the first issue hasn't either. Imagine when instead of one or two events, we discover we haven't resolved fifteen or twenty different wrongs. We end up making a mess of our own lives as well as hurting the person we keep "forgiving." Conditional forgiveness turns our personal relationships into miniature legalistic jurisdictions with the ability to punish the wrongdoer.

This creates a model of behavior that makes us believe that forgiveness is unreachable.

So after a while, we don't even try to forgive. We think, *Why should we, if it doesn't work?* We replace it with toleration or alienation: simply going through the motions and tolerating the hurtful actions or pushing ourselves further from the relationship causing pain. Then the wrongdoer won't care much about trying to change or trying to be forgiven, and the hurtful actions will continue. This isn't what God wants for us in our personal relationships.

God wants us to have the empathy in forgiveness for everyone like I have in Josh. Maybe there is a reason they are acting in anger or resentment. Maybe they are in pain or are having family trouble.

Seeking Forgiveness

Being on the receiving side of forgiveness can be just as hard as, if not even harder than, forgiving someone else. When we seek forgiveness from someone we have wronged, we are vulnerable. We take every ounce of pride and lay it out on the table. Once we have exposed ourselves as the wrongdoer, then the only thing we can do is wait: wait for a response, for our forgiveness, for our sign that everything is going to be okay.

The wait is often what makes us feel powerless. What is the other person going to say or do? Are things going to be right again? How much will they penalize us for similar offenses? Will they answer at all? If they do forgive us, how genuine is it really going to be? The wait and its process are why we can find it so difficult just to stop and say, "I'm sorry."

Josh slowly developed the drive to be more independent. It got to be easier for him to get his own food and drinks than it did to try to request them with his pictures or signs.

One day, Josh was evidently very thirsty. I was in the family room on the couch when I heard a crash and the sound of breaking glass. It came from the kitchen.

"Joshua!" I ran into the kitchen and came to a screeching halt. A glass had fallen and shattered on the floor.

"Eeyooo!" Josh sounded sad and looked as if he was going to cry.

"Oh, buddy," I sighed as I went to grab the broom. I turned to start sweeping to find Joshua picking up the glass pieces with his bare hands and throwing them into the trash.

"Joshy, stop!" I raised my voice, but he continued to pick up the glass.

"Oooo. Eeyooo," he said as he picked up more glass. He paused, stood, and examined his bloody hand without a tear.

"Oh, Josh." I quickly began sweeping the pieces toward the corner so I could kneel and he would be able to walk to me.

"My goodness, guy." I pulled him to me. He sat on my knee and put his head on my shoulder, holding his hand. I picked him up, sat him on the counter by the sink, and cleaned the blood from his injury.

I checked out his hand. There were only a few small scratches. Josh had felt so bad about breaking the glass that he was trying to clean it up on his own. He knew he was wrong, even if it was an accident. He was trying to make things right again.

"Are you okay?" I asked. Josh turned his head and gave me a kiss, and then he gave me the juice pitcher.

I know that I have plenty of bad days and that I need a second chance. Josh is typically a forgiving little boy. I know I have made mistakes and said or done things out of anger. Even Josh understands when I apologize and show him a loving tone, and he forgives me.

Forgiving Ourselves

Guilt can be a useful emotion. It is often God speaking through our conscience. It guides us in deciphering right and wrong, helps us choose better paths, and allows us to recognize when we have hurt someone else. Guilt can even build a sense of charity in those not willing to give altruistically. Too much guilt is counterproductive. It causes an individual to withdraw from others and enter a depressive state. With one individual in a relationship always drenched in guilt, it tips the balance of power and can cause an unhealthy marionette-type relationship.

When we have done something wrong, we often feel guilty. Our sense of guilt will pull us back on the path, and we will usually seek out the person we have wronged to apologize. This is all God's intention in giving us feelings of conviction. However, we tend to hang onto it much longer than is healthy for us. Just as we ask others to forgive us, we have to forgive ourselves for the same wrongdoing.

No, we are not acting godlike in doing this, we are accepting his grace and believing his word. To hold onto our guilt after we have asked for forgiveness is to say that we don't believe God is capable of forgiving us.

About ten months after I left Lyman, the divorce was final. I still held onto a lot of resentment and personal guilt over the demise of my marriage. It wasn't a smooth separation, and I still replayed the last few nights we lived in the same house, over and over again. I felt guilty. And although everything was final, I still felt torn.

December 18, 2004

I found the divorce papers in the mail today. They were stamped and signed by the judge. I am officially a free woman. The funny thing is, I don't feel so free.

I think the four of us are doing so much better, though. Josh is responding more at school and will request his favorite objects with pictures. Mona likes living closer to her friends. Noah likes the new sitter. I have a job that pays well now. We're adjusting quite nicely.

I just wish that when I closed my eyes, I could stop seeing Lyman yelling at me, screaming at me that there is no way I was leaving, and regarding me no higher than property. Yelling at me over and over that this is wrong. "It wouldn't be what God would want," he would say. That might be true, but I couldn't stay. I've told him I'm sorry and that there was no other way I could manage.

I know I did everything I could to try to make our relationship work. I tried to forget our problems and work through them, but things only got worse. I can only heal as fast as I can heal. There is no rushing or changing my feelings. Building love out of anger is impossible as a couple. I couldn't stand going through the motions anymore. I know I did what I could. I tried. I failed.

I know that God never intended for couples to get divorced, but there were a lot of issues in our marriage that God never intended or condoned. I wrestled with and prayed about what I was supposed to do. Stay or go? I was tired of being hurt all of the time; I wasn't sure leaving was what God wanted for me, but I knew he would forgive me and be able, regardless, to use what was left for his will. I asked God to forgive me. I know Lyman never will.

I hear about it every time the phone rings or he comes to pick up the kids. I'm tired of hearing how wrong I am. I am over the confusion. I am through with nightmares and the upset stomach. If God can forgive me, certainly I can't hold this against myself forever. I used to wonder if I would ever feel free again. Today, I know I am.

We can't control how others are going to react; we can only control our own responses. We can't force someone to apologize, but we always have the option of forgiving him. We can't mandate someone accept our apology, but what counts is that we try. Often, this absence of acknowledgment creates undue guilt. If we ask, God forgives us. When we accept his forgiveness, we forgive ourselves and move forward. Even if our apology is not accepted, the cycle is always complete because God always forgive those who seek his forgiveness.

The cycle of forgiveness is a beautiful check-and-balance system for our imperfect earthly relationships. If each segment is used appropriately, it offers a harmonizing effect on power struggles and examining wrongdoing. It is effective even if at different times in a relationship there is only one person running the cycle. Often, it is this way with Joshua.

In order to be an effective parent to Joshua, I have to be able to forgive. For my forgiveness to be real, I have to make sure it is not contingent on Josh behaving himself from that point in time. That would be a ridiculous expectation for Joshua. I have to take every event on its own in order for him to learn different behavior. I strive for our mother-son relationship to mimic the way that God forgives us.

Joshua also made me realize how difficult this is to apply to other people in my life, but also to know that is what God intended for us to do. He knows we will ask forgiveness on several occasions, but he never holds our past against us. God's forgiveness isn't until we screw up again, it is always.

God wants us to forgive as well. God is there for us in spirit and always in prayer while we grieve and reconcile our troubles and learn to forgive. To be unable to forgive is not to trust fully that everything is in God's hands and that he is capable of using it for his plan. Looking back on my life with Joshua thus far, I see how we couldn't be at this happier point without both good and bad events working together for him.

In my journey with Josh, I have discovered how much I rely on God to help me forgive others. I remember all of the thoughts I have about Joshua, how often I was frustrated with therapists and teachers. I know how defensive I can get when I feel he is being ridiculed or ignored. I have to be able to forgive people for staring or snickering or for not understanding. I have to forgive them even if they don't know (or care) that they did anything wrong. If I can't, I carry that negative energy with me, which will unfavorably affect how I am able to control my thoughts and actions.

Joshua taught me not only how to forgive and let go, but also how to ask for forgiveness and be more aware of where I go wrong. God will always forgive us. We are never unforgivable. He never forgives us with stipulations attached. Even though we may remember everything we have done wrong, if we ask, it has been wiped clean. We always get a fresh start with him, even when no one else in the world would give us a chance. And when forgiveness in our relationships gets too confusing, this is the easiest place in the cycle to start.

CHAPTER 14

"So in everything, do to others what you would have them do to you." Matthew 7:12 (NIV)

SIDE EFFECTS

Side effects are often associated with medicine. Media inundates us with pharmaceutical commercials telling us all sorts of horrible side effects that can be associated with a medicine that has the ability to change the outlook of a life for the better. The difficult part is weighing the risks and the benefits to decide if taking a medication is worth experiencing the possible disadvantages of the drug.

I never wanted to medicate Joshua. I always thought he was so young, and I worried how damaging some of the drugs the doctor was suggesting could be to him. As he grew older, he behaviorally became more and more challenging. I began reading about different vitamin regimens that could provide some benefits. I tried adding cod liver oil to his juices and experienced some great results. He was more attentive and slower to anger. I was satisfied using a more natural solution to Josh's issues for a while. Unfortunately, the results did nothing for his sleep issues. After one horrible night, refraining from medication was no longer a choice.

Josh had been in and out of fits all evening. I put his brother and sister to bed and brought him in my room to watch a movie, hoping he would calm down. He seemed to be full of energy. He finally went down for bed around one in the morning. I turned off the television and left him in his makeshift bed on the floor. I crawled into my bed to catch what sleep I could before he awoke again.

Shortly after three, he jumped up and was galloping around the room, screaming and biting his hand. He began hopping up and down on his knees. He continued to scream. I got out of bed and stooped down at his level.

"Joshy. What is wrong? Did you have a bad dream?" I kept my arms outstretched as he paced and screamed, hoping he would give me a hug and calm himself.

He did approach me after a few more laps of the room. I wrapped my arms around him and stroked his back. He sobbed.

"It's okay … Ouch!" He bit my shoulder. I pushed him away and grabbed the remote control. I turned his movie on. He was still crying.

I lay down on his floor bed and patted the pillow next to me. He sobbed but came and stretched out in his bed. I covered him and he quietly watched *Monsters Inc.* until he appeared to doze into sleep, and so did I.

"Eeeyeoowwww!" I awoke to a horrendous screech. I wasn't sure what I had heard. I lifted my head to see Josh's figure in the light of the television, running full speed toward me. He leaped into the air and landed smack on my backside. I heard a loud pop. Josh was scared silent and holding his arm. He rocked back and forth, grimacing and trying to go to sleep. I lifted my torso toward Josh, who was now sitting back on his blanket, but as I turned to check his arm, I quickly realized that it wasn't Joshua who was injured.

The pain flooded my lower back. I pushed myself up slowly into a standing position, inch by inch, becoming harder and harder to stand. Once upright, the pain seemed to dissipate a little. I made my way to the bathroom and sat on the toilet. I realized right then that the pop I had heard was definitely my tailbone.

After that night and a cortisone shot at the doctor the next day, I suddenly saw how vulnerable I really was. I knew I could not always be available twenty-four hours a day and be on the top of my game. I was scared when I thought of how long I could be trying to heal. How was I going to get through the day? I could hardly walk and definitely couldn't sit. How was I going to take care of everyone? How would I take care of Josh? I had been doing so well to keep my delicate balancing act going. I just never realized how fragile it was. One wrong move and I had to drop everything.

I seriously considered how Josh would do on medication for the first time that evening. I was cooking dinner. The shot had only taken the edge off the pain, and I was still very sore. ("A definite sign of a cracked tailbone," my doctor said.) The kids were moving at speeds faster than I was. I put their food on plates and lay down on the couch. Mona and Noah sat to eat, but Josh had a free-for-all. He couldn't sit and even focus to eat a meal. He would take a bite and run through the room, making passes over his plate every now and then. I was tired just watching him. I knew we would need medication to induce sleep, but I also pondered if it could help him in other areas as well.

Medication is a touchy issue with parents. It often instills a gut-wrenching feeling of guilt in parents. It offers a chemical solution for their problems. I tried very hard to keep Josh off medication, but when I understood that I wouldn't be able to safely care for Josh without it, I knew I had no other options. The possible side effects of medicating Joshua paled in comparison to the effects of not medicating him. If he could crack a tailbone without trying, what would happen if he got really mad? What could he do to himself? What would happen when he was bigger? I was growing tired and needed to make sure that he slept soundly at night so that he wouldn't hurt himself or anyone else.

And so began the journey that seems to never end. What medicines do I try? How much should he take? It becomes a gentle dance between doctors and pharmacists and actual practice. What should work doesn't always work, and even the doctors don't agree. At the age of seven, Josh had already ingested more pills and as many different prescriptions as I had in all my years. I could see some weren't going to work after a few days. Our problems would worsen and he would become more obsessive. Other times, some of the medicines were effective for a while, but their benefits would taper or he would need more and more pills for them to remain effective. If the doctor wanted to switch meds, it was often a long process of weaning him off one med and gradually introducing another. Sometimes, it feels like Josh is a science fair experiment gone wrong.

I already knew it was going to be a long evening. I guess I just didn't realize how long. Josh and Noah and I had just dropped Mona off at music lessons. We were driving home. Josh had thrown a horrible fit in the music center. I never did figure out what he was trying to tell me, but he was quiet only for the moment. I had already scrapped the trip to the grocery and, foreseeing that Josh was not going to make it, was calling someone to pick up Mona from practice. As I reached for the phone in my purse, I felt a sharp pain in my wrist. Josh was digging his nails into my arm, biting his hand, and banging his head against the car seat. He stopped and I tried to reassure him that we were going home.

Josh was breathing as if he were trying not to cry. I backed the car into the street and shifted into traffic, heading home. He suddenly came over the armrest, still in his seat belt, and grabbed a fistful of hair in his left hand while scratching my neck with his right. I pushed his hand in my hair to my head and steered the car with my free arm. Noah screamed, and I felt Josh's nails dig in further. I firmly told him to stop, and he went back to head banging and hand biting for a minute. I tried to find a place to stop, but I was in the center lane during rush-hour traffic. Before I could even check to switch lanes, I felt my face start to sting, and then I felt another slap and another and another. He grabbed my hair again and pulled me down. I felt teeth on my scalp, but I kept trying to watch the road.

I pushed his body back to the seat. Even in his seat belt, he was still able to reach my seat. He released his hold on my head, and I scooted as close to my window as I could go. It was rush hour. There was nowhere to stop. I was crying now, which made things worse. Josh hates the sound of crying. But I couldn't stop. Neither could Noah, hiding in the back seat. Josh came after me, this time attacking my right arm as I tried to shield my face. Punch after punch, smack after smack, he relentlessly tried to get me to be silent.

Finally, we were stopped at a red light. I was able to catch his hands and pull his arms across his chest. He was squawking. I bound his arms into my right hand and dialed the cell with my left. I reached my father but was hardly able to do anything but sob at this point. I tried to explain what was going on and said that I couldn't pick up Mona. I needed him to get her. Immediately, Josh broke loose and popped me in the eye. I started crying harder. My dad tried to see if I was okay.

"Just get Mona, please!" I yelled and hung up the phone. Josh was biting his hand again and throwing himself against the back of the seat.

The light was green again, and there was still no way over to a parking lot or road side. I guess no one noticed I was getting the snot beat out of me. I was even passed by two different police cars, so I guess I was managing to drive straight. I prayed that we made it home in one piece. He started slapping my arm again. It felt wet. I thought he was spitting, but there was blood. I'm not even sure whose it was. His? Mine? The blood must have scared him because he let out a shriek and grabbed my face, cutting my cheek with his nails. My tears stung as they ran into the new scratches.

Then, as we neared home, he stopped. There was an eerie silence. Josh was still. Blood was beading on his right hand in the shape of a bite mark. Noah was terrified, but motionless. I only breathed shallowly. I turned the car into the driveway and opened the garage door. I pulled in swiftly, put the gear in park, and shut off the car. Josh calmly got out of the car and entered the house. He even shut the door. He never shuts the door. That wasn't Joshua.

His brother hopped over the car seat and cradled into my lap, hugging me as softly as he could. Neither one of us said anything for a few minutes. Then Noah opened my door and went into the house. I sat in the car and took a deep breath. I wondered what all the medication was really doing for him or to him. I wondered if I would ever feel like I wasn't playing chemistry set with my child. I breathed again and went inside, ready for round two.

Medication always has an intended result. Unfortunately, the result can vary from person to person, and a medication can give you a very different actual result. With medication, you often have to ask what it is you are trying to accomplish. Josh began taking medication to decrease his activity level and reduce his obsessive-compulsive traits. None of the doctors intended Josh to react the way he did, but it happened, and it had to be corrected.

Our relationships are very similar. Often, we try to achieve a harmonious level in a relationship, and through what we say or do, we can end up with a much different result. Our words and actions are a lot like medicine. They can be soothing, calming, or healing. But when you say or do the wrong thing, or it's taken the wrong way, or it is just too harsh, then they can have some horrible side effects. In our everyday relationships, everything we do has a side effect. Maybe it is good, maybe it is bad, but every statement and action shapes our lives and the lives of those around us. We don't always see ourselves as having that much power, but we do. We have the ability to build up or cut down those around us with our words and actions. And much like deciding whether or not to use medication to ease our ailments, we weigh the side effects of saying things or acting certain ways in our relationships.

We often fudge the truth a little and compliment a friend's outfit that really isn't becoming. We avoid telling a coworker what is really on our mind. We focus on encouraging our kids when they are on the losing end of ball games. We constantly dance around sometimes bitter truth in order to keep good relationships and support the people around us.

I found how much watching my words can work in my world. I have more positive effect in my day if I can stay in a good mood and guide Josh's actions with a smooth tone and positive words. Even when things go sour with Josh and his day, I can control the way it turns out with a calm reaction. How I react can set the tone for the rest of the day. Josh fits my emotions and reactions into his schedule. Not only does he know what is happening, he also knows what reactions to expect to what events. Josh's routine acts as a "medicinal" regimen. With a calm attitude, I can help things run smoothly, but if I can't keep my cool, I can expect some ill side effects.

Josh is a creature of habit. Although he dislikes overscheduling and having too many events without breaks, he does enjoy a predictable routine. His routine is medicinal for him, in that being able to know when bike time is over and when he is going to eat and when he is going to bathe reduces his anxieties. Most of the time, our lives are pretty consistent. I let Josh know what is going on for the day, and it is usually right on. Unfortunately, we have to adjust the schedule now and then. This usually results in a massive meltdown. An unforeseen trip to the doctor can cause a major disruption in the rest of the day. Some days, I pay for it until bedtime.

Josh sleeps although not soon enough for me. I shouldn't complain too much. It was my fault. I forgot I'm not allowed to have a bad day.

All I wanted to do was go to the store. Josh was excited about it at first. He knew where we were going and he seemed so happy. We would have been okay if I hadn't forgotten my debit card. So I had to turn around and head home. We went around the block instead of heading to the store. He was mad. He was screaming and biting his hand. He kicked the seats and thrashed his body around.

I ran inside and grabbed my card. I came back to the car. He was still screaming. He calmed down some as I backed down the drive and headed back to the grocery. But he was off the rest of the trip. We only got half of the items on our list and made a scene in the checkout aisle.

When we got home, it was no better. Nothing I said made any difference. My voice became more aggravated. He was upset about everything. Wrong movie. Wrong dinner. Wrong blanket. He began hitting everyone, and I sent him to his room. I checked on him at medicine time and got him ready for bed. He was still upset and had trouble getting to sleep, even after his medicine.

He hates changes in his schedule and definitely doesn't handle them well. I don't always handle him well, either. It's hard to be happy all the time. I should be more patient, but sometimes I get frustrated, and it is hard to keep a mellow tone.

With Joshua, I can't have him question my intent at all. He has to be able to trust my reactions, and, medicated or not, his moods are based on how well I can keep my cool. He pushes me to keep a positive mindset. The more positive my actions and reactions, the smoother our day goes. I strive to have the results of my actions with him consistently reflect my intent. In my life in general, I try to act intentionally so I can have a positive effect on those around me.

Joshua showed me that small things do matter. Good or bad, they shouldn't be ignored. I want to know that no matter how big or small my actions, they have an effect. How it turns out is up to me.

Everything has a side effect. Every action, every word has an effect. Joshua has made me more cautious with what I say and do, not only with my family, but with other relationships as well. I try to be careful so that the outcome of my reaction matches my intent. Acting or speaking out in anger or frustration can have adverse effects. The hurtful things that we allow to slip out of our mouths can only be combated, not erased. Some effects aren't even immediately recognizable, but they can have long-term damage.

CHAPTER 15

"Wisdom is supreme; therefore get wisdom. Though it cost all you have, get understanding." Proverbs 4:7 (NIV)

UNDERSTANDING: FROM SYMPATHY TO EMPATHY

Being able to place others before ourselves is much easier when we are able to broaden our understanding of others. Often, we sympathize with others, sharing their thoughts or feelings during times of trouble. This is an excellent first step in being able to understand those around us. Sometimes, it is all we can do to help someone else. If we can, we need to strive for something deeper.

In order to understand empathetically, we need to connect more on a mental level. We need to identify with the thoughts and feelings of another person. This can be difficult, as we don't always share the same life experiences. Empathy is the ability to put yourself into someone else's shoes and feel what they might be feeling.

When we empathize, we draw on our own experiences and what we know about a given set of circumstances. If we aren't familiar with aspects of a person's life or the scenario they are in, we may not be able to fully empathize with them. If we have a genuine drive to connect at a deeper level, we can learn empathy. This starts in trying to achieve a deeper understanding. This can be learned through gaining a larger understanding of the person with whom you are trying to connect, and what you don't relate to firsthand, you take at face value. While the struggles may never be your own, you can still hear what they have to say and sympathize.

I work hard to understand Josh. I don't always understand where he is coming from, but I do the best I can. I have a real desire to know what he wants. Eventually, I am able to grasp what he is trying to tell me.

It was one of those late nights. My daughter had gone to bed. Noah had fallen asleep in my bed watching a *Spiderman* cartoon DVD. But Josh wasn't anywhere near winding down. I turned off the television and dressed for bed.

About five minutes later, Josh ran into my room. He was quiet for a moment, and then he grabbed my arm and pulled me to the television.

"You want to watch a video?" I asked, grabbing one of his favorite *Veggie Tales* movies and putting it in.

"Beebee ma," he said.

That wasn't it. He screamed and pushed my hand. I selected a few other movies for him to choose from. He pushed them to the floor. He grabbed my arm. He was pulling me to the bedroom door.

"Beebee ma!" he repeated loudly.

"Do you want juice? Hungry?"

He looked into my eyes and screamed, "Beebee ma! Beebee ma."

By this time, Josh was crying and biting his hand. He was definitely trying to tell me something, using the same few verbal patterns. I just didn't get what he was trying to say.

"Beebee ma. Beebee ma!" he cried. He jumped fiercely up and down on his knees, shaking the floor.

"I don't know, guy. What is it?"

"Beebee ma!"

Josh yelled so loud that he woke up Noah, who had managed to stay asleep until then.

Noah sat straight up from bed and asked, "Hey, what happened to the *Spiderman* cartoon?"

"Beebee ma," Josh said calmly as he crawled into my bed with his brother.

"You want to watch *Spiderman?*" I asked excitedly.

Noah nodded.

Josh signed "more" and whispered, "Beebee ma."

I put the *Spiderman* DVD back on and was amazed. He was trying to talk to me. Even with every ounce of my effort, I couldn't understand him. The boys watched the movie and fell asleep.

My need to understand Josh fuels my persistence in trying to understand him. If I had half of that drive for understanding others, I could be more than just a sympathetic ear in more of my personal relationships. It takes a concentrated effort. If we all worked this hard to understand others, the world would be a more empathetic place to be.

We all have a few people in our lives that we find it easier to reach that empathetic level with than others. We work harder to understand them and spend more time with them than others in our lives. When it comes to trying to sympathize with someone we don't know, we can pass quite a few judgments before we understand their story. I usually find my family and myself on the other side of a huge misunderstanding.

I was lying on my bed on the verge of tears. The banging wouldn't stop. Josh was searching for some sort of pressure to ease a sensory need. He was banging on everything and anything, repeatedly. Smack! Bang on the table. Smack! Slap a stack of books. My head echoed every hit. I covered my head with a pillow and pretended it wasn't happening. I heard Mona run into my room.

"Mom!" She seemed scared as she shook my shoulder. "Mom. The police are knocking on the door!"

I sat up and ran out of my room. I heard Josh banging on something in his room. The door was closed but I knew he was in there. I hadn't lost him and I wasn't sure what else the police would want. I unlocked the top of the door. I removed the key from around my neck and turned the deadbolt. I opened the door cautiously.

"Can I help you?" I asked in confusion.

Two male officers stood outside my door. One was already using his radio to report my presence at my residence. The other policeman spoke to me.

"We were in the neighborhood on another call when we noticed you had a broken window."

I was confused. "A broken window?"

"Yeah," said the dark-haired officer. "And there is a foot in the window. It's not moving."

"What?" I questioned. A foot? My thoughts ran to Joshua.

"Ma'am, do you mind if we come in and check it out?"

I opened the door for them and immediately ran upstairs to check on Josh. I don't remember inviting them in, but the officers followed me up the stairwell.

"Couldn't you hear us knocking? We were knocking for a while. Is everyone okay?"

"Sorry. The doorbell is broken."

I pushed Joshua's door open and found him lying on the floor in a sea of glass. He had kicked through the first pane of his bedroom window. His foot remained elevated and resting comfortably on the second pane of glass. He was motionless.

"Joshy!" I called to him. He giggled as I pulled him up to the bed. I brushed glass from his clothes and laid him on my lap to examine his foot. Not a scratch.

The blond officer stood in the doorway while the other officer checked out the window. He came over to the bed to get a second opinion on the foot.

"So he's okay?" he asked me as he peeked at Josh's foot. The dark-haired policeman reached his hand out to touch his heel. Josh laughed hysterically, leaped up, and pushed past the officer in the doorway.

"I guess," I sighed, shaking my head. I was still trying to digest everything that had happened in the last three minutes.

"So you didn't hear the window break?" the blond officer asked.

"No. I hadn't a clue."

His partner doubted me. "He didn't cry or scream? There was no banging?"

"Well, there is always banging," I tried to explain. I hurried out the door. "I need to follow him."

The officers continued asking questions. The first one came after I shut Josh's door and then locked it.

"You've got an awful lot of locks everywhere."

"I never know what I'm going to need to protect." I was too busy going downstairs to find my son to explain.

The dark-haired officer followed directly behind me. "So you couldn't hear us knocking and you didn't hear him kicking the glass. Where were you, exactly?"

"I was in my room. I had a horrible headache."

"So you were sleeping?" the blond prodded.

"No. I couldn't sleep with all of the banging. I just needed to compose myself for a moment."

"What banging are you talking about?" asked the dark-haired officer.

"He's autistic. He will hit things and push on things. Just for fun."

The police officers looked at each other and then back at me. "Really?"

"Yes. He bangs on things again and again. It gets very loud sometimes."

Just then Josh brought a stack of books over to the kitchen table a few feet from the officers. He let out a sound like a war whoop and began slapping the stack of books on the table. The officers were startled. Josh laughed and continued to karate chop the books with his fists.

"Just like that!" I had to raise my voice to be heard over the racket.

The officers exchanged glances but no words. I'm not sure they could have heard each other anyway.

"This is the noise you heard?" the blond officer asked.

"Yes," I answered. "It's all I've heard. Today, yesterday, and the day before that."

After watching Josh and his unusual book slapping ritual, the police seemed to understand what I was talking about and why I might have shut myself in my room.

"Okay, ma'am," said the dark-haired officer. He was speaking loudly. "If you think you are okay, we'll be going.'

"I'm just dandy," I yelled and shook my head. I led them to the door. Josh's banging was getting louder and louder.

"All right then," the officer said as he left the house. "Have a nice day."

I smiled, waved, and then shut the door. I replaced the top latch and turned the deadbolt. The key went back around my neck.

I'm sure the officers thought I was pretty nonchalant about the situation. Josh reacts unusually when he is hurt. He might breathe heavy or whimper, but he rarely cries when he is in pain. I'm pretty sure the police had a hundred other ideas of what they thought was going on in my house. By the end of their visit, they seemed to be fairly understanding of my situation. How their eyes looked at me changed from the beginning to the end of their visit. To begin with, they were scrutinizing everything in my house and every move I made. When they left, they looked at me in pity. I think they felt sorry for me.

Autism can be very isolating, even when you develop your own way of coping and getting through your day. You do the same couple of routines that get you from morning until night with little or no fits. If you find something that works, you tend to stay with it. You often try not to go out or stick to a few key places. Our family sticks to the same two restaurants, the same grocery store, the same few parks. Our boundaries can be pretty limiting at times.

What makes it even more restrictive is the lack of understanding from strangers. Not being understood can be isolating, too. It is hard talking to parents at school functions or at church. My eyes always have to be on Josh. It is hard to convince someone you are really interested in having a conversation with them when you can't even look them in the eye. Most of the time, I'm not even sure they think I am listening. Often in parental group situations, I end up missing conversations because I have to leave to tend to Josh or they started them without me, assuming I wouldn't want to hear. Even when I am among friends, it becomes a challenge because I usually have to run Josh to the bathroom or chase him. I find it hard to start new relationships and still balance the challenges placed upon my older ones. I just wish that our family left a more accurate first impression.

I feel so left out. I've tried to get to know the other moms here, but it's like we are from different worlds. It's hard to find things in common with these ladies anyway, but I'm always distracted. Josh takes up all of my attention. Even when I'm listening to what they are saying, it is hard to show it. I can't look at them and talk, or I'll lose tabs on Josh. One mom kept repeating her questions until I would answer her while looking directly at her. I know that is what "normal" people do, but when I did look at her, I lost Joshua on the field. He was at second base before I could snag him.

Many times, the boys just can't sit through a whole game and I end up watching Mona through binoculars on the playground. Each game that goes by leaves me more and more alone. I finally quit trying. They don't get it. I'm not sure I'd understand my situation looking from the outside. What's the point? I'm better off in my own little world. Josh does it all the time. Maybe it's not so bad.

Lack of empathy or understanding can also make it difficult for Mona and Noah as well. It is difficult to have play dates or overnight guests at our house. It causes confusion and upsets Joshua, usually to the point of a massive fit because someone is in his house. So often, we have trouble with the customary return of an invitation. Many parents don't understand why, even though I have tried to explain. They think that I am being rude when that is never my intention. I simply do not have the physical space in my house to entertain a guest and combat Josh's feelings of encroachment.

Even when we are invited to spend time at someone else's house, it can still be a very disconnected experience. Unless Josh is asleep, one of two things is guaranteed to happen: We find out that it is an overwhelming environment (too loud, too bright, too breakable) and we have to leave early, or I spend most of my time trying to curtail him and running damage control. Either way, I don't usually get to socialize too much with others. Usually when we are invited once, we aren't invited back.

After living at my current house for about five years, I was finally able to make a few close friends. It took some time because I never got to talk for very long before I would have to chase Joshua or redirect him into another activity. But slowly, I was able to get to know these neighbors, who I was able to consider later as close friends.

It was hard to let someone into my crazy, unpredictable world. I really had to put myself out there and be prepared with a take-it-or-leave-it attitude. Building relationships puts you out there, vulnerable to other people's remarks. They got to know my situation, my strong points, my weak points. Now they are able to be empathetic when things get hard. They are able to help me when I'm having a mental moment, and when they don't understand, they take it as it is and let me tell them about it.

It was slow, but my neighbors worked hard to understand Josh and my world. My neighbors were open with me later and told me how Josh scared them when they first met him. He was loud and energetic, and I was usually chasing him at a full sprint; and when I caught him, Joshua was usually quite angry. They were intimidated.

As they got to know Josh and learned what he liked and disliked and what motivated him, they discovered he was just a lovable little boy. They watched how I handled him when he would get upset. He wasn't so scary after all. In fact, they offered to baby-sit him … more than once!

I can accept the fact that not everybody is going to volunteer to baby-sit Josh, but the feelings originally felt by my good friends are the same feelings that most of the people we meet keep as their impression of Joshua. Exposure is key to gaining understanding. One meeting isn't likely enough to put Joshua in a positive light. I work on getting Josh out as much as possible, to expose him to the world around him. It is good for him to learn how to function in the world, and it is good for other people to learn to be a little more understanding. When neither of those things work out, it give me a chance to practice keeping my cool.

A typical day at the grocery is rarely that. Anywhere my crew goes, we tend to put on quite a show. One day, we had to pick up a prescription and went in the opposite side of the store than we usually did. That was my first mistake.

Our list wasn't too long. I needed about ten things and had to pick up Josh's medicine. Most of my items were around the outside aisles of the store. The whole trip should have been a breeze. *Should* have been.

We entered through the south entrance and picked up the medication. Josh was okay with this until we took a cart with us and left the pharmacy and went into the frozen food aisle. He immediately objected to walking through the store and climbed into the main basket of the cart.

I wasn't going to argue. I had done something different, and Josh was upset before we even had one item in the cart. If riding in the cart cooled him down, I was all for it.

We went through the dairy case. I asked Noah what flavors yogurt he wanted. By the time we had made our choice, Josh had reached a package of cheese sticks, opened the wrapping, and started peeling open the individual sticks.

"Joshy," I whined. He shoved an entire stick of cheese into his mouth before I took the cheese away. I placed the cheese in the front of the cart. Of course he couldn't have grabbed the brand that was on sale.

We continued to the end of the dairy case. I opened the door and chose a gallon of milk at the bottom of the rack. When I stood up, Josh was gone. Mona found him in the meat section. He had selected a package of ham and was busy tapping the corner of the plastic with his finger. I got him to put the ham in the cart. He climbed back into the shopping cart. He picked the ham up and began tapping the corner again.

I asked the other two kids to select a loaf of bread. I followed behind, trying to keep my eye on Joshua. Mona asked me what type of bread I wanted. I looked over to tell her to select a loaf of wheat bread. I suddenly heard a hissing sound.

I looked in the cart. Josh had snagged a two-liter bottle of ginger ale off an end cap. He twisted the top and was chugging it. He had opened it with such haste that it began spewing foam. Josh choked and about a third of the bottle fizzed onto the floor.

I took the bottle and replaced the cap. After I notified an employee, we sheepishly continued through our list. We went down an aisle looking for mayonnaise. Noah was on a mission, reading every label along the way. I helped him find the jar that said "Light." Noah located the jar and handed it to me. I went to place it near Joshua, only to discover that he had decided on seven bottles of

Greek-style salad dressing. I started to remove them from the cart.

"Aaaaagh!" he yelled and clasped my hands.

I looked him dead in the eye, "One, Joshy. One is fine."

He dropped the ham and held the remaining bottle of dressing. At the end of the aisle, he became upset when we tried to go to the produce section instead of going to the checkout aisle. I knew I had thrown off his routine, so I abandoned that idea. I figured if I didn't stop now, I might end up spending much more than I had intended.

Josh was happier when we turned back to the checkout lanes. The line was slightly longer than the others, but I chose the end aisle, the one without candy, to try to reduce his already hyped impulse issues. Noah and Josh started playing a weird peekaboo game to kill time. Noah would peek his eyes into the cart. Josh would respond with a highly unusual yell.

"Aaaaaack!" Josh resonated.

Noah started giggling and tried to peek over the side again.

"Aaaaaack!" Josh became louder and the boys laughed together.

"Aaaaaack!" Josh continued. Noah laughed again.

Josh kept going. He was stuck in a loop now. I had calmed Noah down and pulled him out of the equation, but Josh would not stop. He continued the weird sounds about every eight seconds. I touched my finger to his mouth trying to quiet him, but he kept going, becoming more powerful with each bark.

The lady behind me didn't find it very amusing.

"Can't you make him stop?" she pestered.

I turned to her. "Um, not with any legal methods." I flashed her a look and turned back to Josh. I never turned back around.

He barked until we were through the checkout line and outside the grocery store.

Once Josh starts something, it's hard to get him to stop. Sometimes it's a fit, sometimes it's a quest for food, and other times it's an action that's repeated over and over again. When Josh screams in public and I can't redirect him, I know people are watching. Maybe they are thinking, "What a brat!" or "I can't believe she doesn't do anything about it." I'm never 100 percent sure, but I know that is usually an unsympathetic sentiment by the icy glares.

It used to bother me; not so much anymore. Once in a while, when I'm in a mood of my own, I'll have a smart comment ready for them. Usually, I try to ignore them since that is the better thing to do. I guess it is due in part to my apathy and partly because I get plenty of practice that I'm becoming a pro at being able to block out rude onlookers. I handle it much better than I used to.

What is so hard about accepting Joshua? People stare and they judge, and it hurts. It hurts to think that the full extent of a person's understanding is to feel sorry for me. Someone has to know how I can love him. Someone has to know how I can care so much.

He can be tiring. He can wear me down. Even when I am on my last ounce of patience and want to cry, I always go back to the thought, "What if autism hurts?"

What if Josh is in pain? What if he always has a headache or his eyes constantly hurt? Just existing would be a daily triumph. What if the vacuum actually causes his ears to hurt or that tickle really felt like a slap?

What if the pain isn't only physical? What if his feelings hurt because he can't jibber-jabber about his day like Mona and Noah? What if it pains him to stay silent? What if it hurts him to not say the things he wants to be able to say?

All I can think is that it is my duty as his mother to make it feel better. It is my joy to love him and soothe him when I can. And on those days when I have no more nerves to hold onto, I help him out of pity until the feeling is replaced once again with love.

Feeling sorry for someone is a very humane emotion. It reminds you that even those you aren't close to (and sometimes those you are) are human and deserving of concern. Pity is the basic emotion behind sympathy. With a willingness to feel further, we can build a need for empathy for others in our lives. We can work on having that greater understanding for others, and what we can't understand, we can take at face value, remembering that everything is in God's hands and that he has a place for everyone.

One summer evening, Josh was riding his bike in our cul-de-sac. He loved to ride and had amazing coordination and awareness of things around him when he was riding. Unfortunately, one of our neighbors had a guest. There was an unfamiliar truck parked in Josh's riding area.

He spun around the driveway, and even though he tried to turn, he was a split second too late. His hand brake scraped along the side of the truck, flipping the bike to its side and leaving a three-inch scratch in the navy blue paint. Josh stood up immediately and walked into our house.

Guessing he was fine when he returned with a picture book, I checked out the damage. My heart sunk when I saw the scratch. I knew I couldn't afford to fix it, and the mark wouldn't rub off. I couldn't pretend it didn't happen. That just wasn't right.

My friends kept an eye on Josh while I went to report the accident to the unknown truck owners. I was nervous. I knocked on my neighbor's door and told her what had happened. The truck belonged to her father-in-law. She checked the damage herself and then invited me in to tell him the story.

I introduced myself and began to tell Josh's plight.

"I'm really sorry. He usually steers so well, but he just didn't make it. If you need me to get it repaired, I will." That last sentence didn't come out so smoothly.

"Is he okay?" the man asked.

"He's fine," I answered.

"Well, then. That's what matters," he responded without hesitating.

I was shocked. "Are you sure you don't want to take a look at the truck?"

My neighbor, who had looked at the car, described the scratch. He still insisted that it was nothing and told me again that he was glad Josh was okay. I was stunned. I apologized again and thanked him profusely.

My neighbor's father-in-law offered the ultimate example of genuine forgiveness and understanding. He had only seen Joshua for about five seconds when he pulled into the driveway and walked into the house, yet he was accepting of Josh and his condition. Even when there was a problem, he understood that it wasn't intentional and knew I had no control over what had happened. His first concern was for Joshua and his well-being, demonstrating the worth of the human spirit no matter what the package. It was also a beautiful realization that while Josh can challenge some to judge too quickly, he also brings out the best in others.

To learn to empathize is to banish judgment. We are supposed to love our neighbor whether they drive a Lexus or have to walk, whether they are healthy or ill, happy or cranky. Josh challenged me to see how often I categorize others. I learned to be not so quick to judge. You never know what they went through that month or even that morning. And in working so hard to understand him and the autism at his level, I found that the process translated to many people who aren't affected by autism. The more I am able to empathize and sympathize, the more I can truly love others the way that God wants me to and the more I can reflect his love through my life.

CHAPTER 16

"Many are the plans in a man's heart, but it is the Lord's purpose that prevails." Proverbs 19:21 (NIV)

PURPOSE

When we are younger, we hear the question asked again and again, "What do you want to be when you grow up?" I knew. I knew exactly what I was going to be. I planned on being a world-renowned mystery writer. I would have a column in the *New York Times,* and I would travel around the United States, going on talk shows and promoting my new novels. Of course, I would always save time for my cameo appearances on *Law and Order*. And if that didn't work out, I would be a comedian.

Needless to say, I am not a famous novelist. I don't write for a newspaper, and I haven't even been in the audience of a talk show, let alone a featured guest. I haven't left my home state in two years, and I can't even watch a full episode of *Law and Order* without interruption. Although there are times my life feels as if it is one gigantic cosmic joke, I'm not sure it classifies me as a comedian. I have fulfilled none of what my passionate young heart set out to complete as my life's purpose.

What my pre-Joshua self did not understand is that passion and purpose do not always go together. We all have our passions, those things we love to fill our days with and hope we can make a life's work out of them. We try to make them our life's purpose, our reason for getting out of bed in the morning. We all want to leave something behind. We spend much of our life seeking this out, some idea of how we want to be remembered when we're gone. A legacy.

We have so many things we would love to do and maybe continue to try to do, but as much as we try, it may not be what was intended for our life. Many people spend their lives running after their passions, and even though they thought they were enjoying themselves, later they find out that something is missing. Finding purpose involves accepting change readily and understanding that your desires and dreams may not be in line with what God has in mind for you. To find your true purpose is to be able to let go and let God lead you to where you need to be.

I guess it wasn't all that high: two stories, maybe three in some places. I just hated the idea of being suspended on a thin cable far above the amusement park, seated on a metal bench with only a free-swinging bar in front of me. I hated the Sky Ride.

Josh wanted to ride it. I tried to get him excited about rides he had loved just the year before: the Tilt-a-whirl, the Scrambler, the Snowcaps. He showed no interest. He wanted to go on the Sky Ride. So we did.

Our family goes to the amusement park every year. Mona and Noah had tried to get me to ride it the year before. I refused and let them ride together. I piggybacked Josh and we ran across the park, with Mona and Noah riding above us all the way to the other side. It made sense at the time. I wasn't about to go on that ride … until now.

Josh wasn't into the rides like he was the year before. Every thing he enjoyed previously, caused him to cry. The only thing he had wanted to do so far was the merry-go-round. That was fine except if I spun one more time, I was going to be shorted my breakfast. I walked him to the other side of the park as a distraction. Josh found the stairs to the Sky Ride.

I chased him up the stairs all the way to the top.

"Josh," I encouraged, "I don't think you really want to go on this one."

Josh started cooing. He looked me straight in the eye and signed, "Please—more—please."

I couldn't say no to that. I made my way to the top of the stairs. The ride attendant positioned us in front of a cart. Josh hopped on immediately and shut his bar. I was nervous, but had no choice but to do the same.

I felt the cart dip and swing as I lifted my feet and shut my bar. I grabbed Josh's bar to make sure it stayed shut the entire way. I closed my eyes tightly. The wire hummed as the cart was pulled along the cable. I said a silent prayer for our safety and then opened my eyes when I heard Josh laugh.

He seemed to love the Sky Ride. He was wide eyed as he looked around the park and then down over the side of our cart. I couldn't see his face anymore. I had no idea if he really liked this. If he decided to throw a fit, we were done for. The only place to land was the pavement or the blazing hot metal rooftops of the buildings along the boardwalk. Neither seemed like a good option. He pulled his head up again.

He was smiling and scanning over the landscape. The wheel on our cart hit a bump. My body shook. It was all normal. They had to attach the cables for the ride somewhere, but it didn't put me at ease. He swung his leg back and forth as he giggled. Our cart rocked.

"Joshy, stop," I gasped, placing my hand on his knee.

He stopped and put his hand over mine. I thought he was going to push the bar open, but he seemed to sense that I was scared. He was calmer than usual and more alert. He looked at me intently, leaned toward my cheek, and gave me a very gentle kiss. I grinned at him. Josh patted my hand and laughed.

I took a deep breath and actually enjoyed the rest of the ride. Joshua has a gift. He can get me try to do things that I wouldn't do under any other circumstances and make me feel good about it. Joshua has made me overcome all sorts of fears: fear of falling, fear of failure, fear of ridicule, fear of loss, fear of weakness, fear of the unknown. They are all gone. Raising Joshua has made me fearless.

As Joshua and I traveled along the skyline, I felt that feeling I've had with him so many times before: the peace that comes from knowing I was riding in God's hands.

Inside that feeling of peace lies my life's purpose. I fully acknowledge that my life is not my own, and I seek every day to live for what God wants in my life. Joshua showed me how even though I didn't exactly end up where I thought I would, God does nothing by accident. Discovering God's purpose for you is often a molding process. He bends and shapes you and has you where you are supposed to be. There is a purpose behind every apparent problem or setback. When things are challenging, there is always a lesson that comes out of weakness.

Joshua has taught me how to live fully, intentionally, and with passion. He has shown me how loving and serving others is a way to connect to God. My legacy is in what I can do and give to other people. Through Joshua, God made me recognize my true purpose. Joshua stands as an example of what God has done for me in my life, in hopes that others can see what he can do for theirs.

Chapter 17

> "By wisdom a house is built, and through understanding it is established." Proverbs 24:3 (NIV)

WISDOM

Wisdom is the intuitive discernment between right and wrong as it pertains to actions and insights. It involves the ability to be selfless and have a deeper understanding of what is true. We gain wisdom as a result of living life. It is the sum of our experiences, mistakes, consequences, and successes.

Life is a continual journey and learning process. We never stop learning and changing and growing. Sometimes, the lessons we are to be examining and studying aren't always so obvious, especially when we complicate our lives materially and neglect them spiritually. As we grow in age, we also hope to grow in wisdom. We hope we learn from our mistakes and develop that common sense that comes from experiencing life.

Joshua accentuated this process for me. He made it easier to see what was really important in life. Josh's very being forced me to slow down and realize the gifts that God has given me. Josh is a blessing. He has so much to show people. Everyone has a story. Everyone can be a teacher. We often cross paths with several people who mentor us and guide us. There are other people who I admire, but Joshua is one of my most influential teachers.

Living with Josh made me slow down and refocus. I had to examine my expectations for him, my family, and myself. I had to align them with God's expectations. I had to concentrate on the little miracles instead of waiting for one big one. With every accomplishment that I make with Joshua, he is moving closer to the goals we set. Every little piece of a puzzle contributes to the big picture. Each milestone is progress. A journey is easier when you can celebrate each small step on the way to the final destination.

Josh has made me more humble and understanding of others, both with and without disabilities. I learned what it was to forgive honestly and completely. I discovered how to be a more forgiving and loving person. Joshua has molded me to be more patient and to keep going even when things get difficult.

Josh has given me the wisdom to spend every day being better. I have good days and bad days, but I keep trying to improve. I try to give more, try harder, enjoy more, worry less, and just be better. Joshua has shown me how to not take the little things for granted and to live my life with passion even if I am doing something highly ordinary.

I know my adventures with Joshua aren't through, and neither are the lessons he has to teach me. Recently, when I was dealing with a laughing Joshua, locked inside my car with my keys and a bag of candy, I was reminded that life with Josh will never be quiet, only quieter. It will be a dynamic flow of events waxing and waning through the triumphant and failing, the joyous and sorrowful, the furious and the commonplace.

Today, I can watch in sheer amazement as Josh plays with his siblings and neighbors. When I reflect back on Josh as an infant and as he grew, I see how really difficult things were. I see how much sleep I missed and am astonished that any of my family is here today. I operated literally and figuratively half-awake. When I look at how far Josh has come, I see God.

Josh is markedly better now than when he was a preschooler. He focuses more. He can sit and work for defined periods. He can use crayons and pencils to scribble. He listens to directions and follows them (the majority of time). He plays within boundaries and runs off less frequently. He can follow a cart through a store trip. He can eat with a spoon (but needs consistent reminders). He starts his own bath and appropriately adjusts the water temperature. He can swim and tread water. He uses the toilet and sleeps through the night (98 percent of nights). He likes to help cook and plays more often with his brother and sister. He is even developing a heightened awareness for cars. He has an untapped capacity to love.

If I was told when he was three that he would get to where he is today, I wouldn't have believed you. It was a grueling process; Josh is much better off than he was years ago. I watch him play and ride his bike with a sense of hesitant relief. I am proud of how far we have come, but I know our journey isn't over. He isn't finished, and I still have so much more to learn.

When Josh rides his bike, he occasionally hops off and runs to the grass. He will tilt his head to the left, look up, smile, and giggle like he sees an old friend. He would do it when he was a toddler, too. That is one thing that has never changed. Doctors say he is in a trance, looking at reflections of light. Some thought he could even be hallucinating. His aunt says he's laughing with angels. I'm not entirely sure what he finds so interesting up there. Maybe, just maybe, he is hearing God whisper.